LENTEN
GOSPEL
REFLECTIONS

BISHOP ROBERT BARRON
with reflection questions by Peggy Pandaleon

WORD on FIRE

WORD ON FIRE CATHOLIC MINISTRIES
www.WORDONFIRE.org

✠
Introduction

Friends,

Thank you for joining me as we journey together toward the great feast of Easter!

Lent is a season for refocusing on the suffering and death of our Lord Jesus Christ, so that we will be ready to embrace the good news of the Resurrection.

Why this emphasis on suffering? Because Christ saved us through an act of suffering. He bore in his own person the weight of our sin and died for us on the cross, where suffering and love coincided.

And the Church is the Body of Christ, which participates in Christ. Therefore, we shouldn't be surprised that we will be called upon to suffer out of love. In the economy of grace, God may use our suffering to bear the burden of another member of the Body of Christ, just as one system can take up the work of another, or one organ can support another.

So as we begin with Ash Wednesday, let us resolve to focus on Christ's suffering, and to unite our own suffering—through fasting, prayer, almsgiving, and reflection on the Stations of the Cross—with the suffering members of the Church. It is not the destination but the journey that will ultimately transform us.

Peace,

+ Robert Barron

Bishop Robert Barron

LENTEN
GOSPEL
REFLECTIONS

Wednesday, February 17, 2021

Ash Wednesday

Jesus said to his disciples:
"Take care not to perform righteous deeds in order that people may see them; otherwise, you will have no recompense from your heavenly Father. When you give alms, do not blow a trumpet before you, as the hypocrites do in the synagogues and in the streets to win the praise of others. Amen, I say to you, they have received their reward. But when you give alms, do not let your left hand know what your right is doing, so that your almsgiving may be secret. And your Father who sees in secret will repay you.

"When you pray, do not be like the hypocrites, who love to stand and pray in the synagogues and on street corners so that others may see them. Amen, I say to you, they have received their reward. But when you pray, go to your inner room, close the door, and pray to your Father in secret. And your Father who sees in secret will repay you.

"When you fast, do not look gloomy like the hypocrites. They neglect their appearance, so that they may appear to others to be fasting. Amen, I say to you, they have received their reward. But when you fast, anoint your head and wash your face, so that you may not appear to be fasting, except to your Father who is hidden. And your Father who sees what is hidden will repay you."

Friends, today's Gospel prescribes the disciplines of prayer, fasting, and almsgiving. I want to speak about the biblical principle behind almsgiving. I know I've quoted to you before some of the breathtaking remarks of saints and popes. For example, Pope Leo XIII said, "Once the demands of necessity and propriety have been met, the rest of your money belongs to the poor." St. John Chrysostom said—and St. Ambrose echoed him—"For the man who has two shirts in his closet, one belongs to him; the other belongs to the man who has no shirt." These ideas are, of course, rooted in the biblical prophets, who continually rail against those who are indifferent to the poor.

Compassion is key to Christian ethics, learning to suffer with and feel with the other. We're not dealing with an abstract Aristotelian moral philosophy, but rather with something more visceral.

This is precisely why the two great commandments are so tightly linked: "Love the Lord your God with all your heart . . . and love your neighbor as yourself." In loving God, you feel the feelings of

7

God, and God is compassionate to the poor and oppressed. That's all the argument that a biblical person needs.

REFLECT: How do you think the practices of Lent, specifically prayer, almsgiving, and fasting, can lead us to a deeper relationship with Christ?

_____

_____

_____

_____

_____

_____

_____

_____

_____

_____

_____

_____

_____

_____

_____

Thursday, February 18, 2021

Thursday after Ash Wednesday

LUKE 9:22-25

Jesus said to his disciples:
"The Son of Man must suffer greatly and be rejected by the elders, the chief priests, and the scribes, and be killed and on the third day be raised."

Then he said to all, "If anyone wishes to come after me, he must deny himself and take up his cross daily and follow me. For whoever wishes to save his life will lose it, but whoever loses his life for my sake will save it. What profit is there for one to gain the whole world yet lose or forfeit himself?"

Friends, our Gospel today from Luke lays out Jesus' conditions for discipleship: "If anyone wishes to come after me, he must deny himself and take up his cross daily and follow me. For whoever wishes to save his life will lose it, but whoever loses his life for my sake will save it."

How do we overcome pain? How do we attain joy? Not from a Stoic resignation, nor from a Buddhist negation of the self, nor from a Platonic contemplation of the eternal forms, but rather from the sacrifice of the self in love. Jesus is going to Jerusalem in order to give himself away, to sacrifice himself in love for the other—and in this, he will become a source of life to others.

Ronald Knox talked about the sign of the cross this way: the first two gestures form the letter "I" and the next two cross it out. That's what the cross of Jesus meant and means. The path of discipleship is the path of self-sacrificing love—and that means the path of suffering.

REFLECT: How do you "lose your life" or deny yourself for the sake of Christ?

_____

_____

_____

_____

_____

_____

_____

_____

_____

_____

_____

Friday, February 19, 2021

Friday after Ash Wednesday

MATTHEW 9:14-15

The disciples of John approached Jesus and said, "Why do we and the Pharisees fast much, but your disciples do not fast?" Jesus answered them, "Can the wedding guests mourn as long as the bridegroom is with them? The days will come when the bridegroom is taken away from them, and then they will fast."

Friends, in today's Gospel, people ask Jesus why his disciples do not fast. He says that as wedding guests they will not fast while he, the Bridegroom, is with them. But "the days will come," he says, "when the bridegroom is taken away from them, and then they will fast."

Why do we fast? Because we have a hunger for God, which is the deepest hunger. We're meant to get access to that hunger. We're meant to feel it so that it can direct us toward God. Every spiritual master recognizes the danger that if we allow the superficial hunger of our lives to dominate, we never reach the deepest hunger.

Thomas Merton once observed that our desires for food and drink are something like little children in their persistence and tendency to dominate. Unless and until they are disciplined, they will skew the functions of the soul according to their purposes.

And fasting is a way of disciplining the hunger for food and drink. It is a way of quieting those desires by not responding to them immediately, so that the deepest desires emerge. Unless you fast you might never realize how hungry you are for God.

REFLECT: Why do we fast during Lent? How does this practice affect you?

_____

_____

_____

_____

_____

_____

_____

_____

_____

_____

_____

_____

Saturday, February 20, 2021

Saturday after Ash Wednesday

LUKE 5:27–32

Jesus saw a tax collector named Levi sitting at the customs post. He said to him, "Follow me." And leaving everything behind, he got up and followed him. Then Levi gave a great banquet for him in his house, and a large crowd of tax collectors and others were at table with them. The Pharisees and their scribes complained to his disciples, saying, "Why do you eat and drink with tax collectors and sinners?" Jesus said to them in reply, "Those who are healthy do not need a physician, but the sick do. I have not come to call the righteous to repentance but sinners."

Friends, in today's Gospel, Jesus tells Matthew, "Follow me." The call of Jesus addresses the mind, but it is meant to move through the mind into the body, and through the body into the whole of one's life, into the most practical of moves and decisions. "Follow me" has the sense of "apprentice to me" or "walk as I walk; think as I think; choose as I choose." Discipleship entails an entire reworking of the self according to the pattern and manner of Jesus.

Upon hearing the address of the Lord, the tax collector, we are told, "got up and followed him." The Greek word behind "got up" is *anastas*, the same word used to describe the Resurrection (*anastasis*) of Jesus from the dead. Following Jesus is indeed a kind of resurrection from the dead, since it involves the transition from a lower form of life to a higher, from a preoccupation with the temporary goods of this world to an immersion in the goodness of God.

Those who have undergone a profound conversion tend to speak of their former life as a kind of illusion, something not entirely real. Thus Paul can say, "I live, no longer I, but Christ lives in me"; Thomas Merton can speak of the "false self" that has given way to the authentic self; and perhaps most movingly, the father of the prodigal son can say, "This son of mine was dead, and has come to life again; he was lost, and has been found."

REFLECT: With what "temporary goods of this world" are you overly preoccupied? What is Christ asking you to do about that preoccupation?

_____

_____

_____

_____

_____

_____

Sunday, February 21, 2021

First Sunday of Lent

MARK 1:12-15

The Spirit drove Jesus out into the desert, and he remained in the desert for forty days, tempted by Satan. He was among wild beasts, and the angels ministered to him.

After John had been arrested, Jesus came to Galilee proclaiming the gospel of God: "This is the time of fulfillment. The kingdom of God is at hand. Repent, and believe in the gospel."

Friends, in today's Gospel, Jesus goes into Galilee and begins to preach. The first words out of his mouth, as Mark reports them, serve as a sort of summary statement of his life and work: "This is the time of fulfillment. The kingdom of God is at hand. Repent, and believe in the gospel."

The moment has arrived, the privileged time, the *kairos*; something that human beings have been longing for and striving after and hoping to see has appeared, and the time is now for a decision, for action. Jesus' very first words are a wake-up call, a warning bell in the night, a summons to attention. This is not the time to be asleep, not the time to be languishing in complacency and self-satisfaction, not the time for delaying tactics, for procrastination and second guessing.

In the Byzantine liturgy, we find the oft-repeated call to "be attentive," and in the Buddhist tradition, there is a great emphasis placed on wakefulness. In the fiction of James Joyce, we often find that moments of spiritual insights are preceded by a great thunderclap, the cosmic alarm shocking the characters (and the reader) into wide-awakeness. The initial words of Jesus' first sermon are a similar invitation to psychological and spiritual awareness: there is something to be seen, so open your eyes!

REFLECT: Is there anything that you have been putting off that you believe Jesus wants you to do? What can you do this week to address your procrastination?

_____

_____

_____

_____

_____

_____

_____

_____

Monday, February 22, 2021

Feast of the Chair of Saint Peter the Apostle

MATTHEW 16:13-19

When Jesus went into the region of Caesarea Philippi he asked his disciples, "Who do people say that the Son of Man is?" They replied, "Some say John the Baptist, others Elijah, still others Jeremiah or one of the prophets." He said to them, "But who do you say that I am?" Simon Peter said in reply, "You are the Christ, the Son of the living God." Jesus said to him in reply, "Blessed are you, Simon son of Jonah. For flesh and blood has not revealed this to you, but my heavenly Father. And so I say to you, you are Peter, and upon this rock I will build my Church, and the gates of the netherworld shall not prevail against it. I will give you the keys to the Kingdom of heaven. Whatever you bind on earth shall be bound in heaven; and whatever you loose on earth shall be loosed in heaven."

LENTEN *GOSPEL* REFLECTIONS

Friends, today's Gospel spells out the importance of Peter's confession. For it is upon this inspired confession that the Church is built. Not, mind you, on popular opinion, which is shifting and indecisive, and not on personal holiness, which is all too rare. It is built upon the inspired authority of Peter—and I say, "Thank God!"

We make this troubling and extraordinary claim that it is through a special charism of the Spirit that Peter and his successors govern the Church. Now, I realize that I have many Protestant readers and that this text has been, between Catholics and Protestants, a stumbling block. Let me clarify what is and is not at stake here.

What is the focus of Peter's confession? It has to do with who Jesus is. This is the rock upon which the Church is built. We don't say for a moment that all of Peter's practical decisions are right, that everything he says is right. But we are saying that he is right about who Jesus is: a man who is also the Son of the living God. And this is the source and ground of the whole operation.

REFLECT: How would you answer Jesus' question: "Who do you say that I am?" What do Peter's words "the Christ" and "the Son of the living God" mean in your own understanding?

Tuesday, February 23, 2021

First Week of Lent

MATTHEW 6:7-15

Jesus said to his disciples: "In praying, do not babble like the pagans, who think that they will be heard because of their many words. Do not be like them. Your Father knows what you need before you ask him

"This is how you are to pray:

Our Father who art in heaven,
hallowed be thy name,
thy Kingdom come,
thy will be done,
on earth as it is in heaven.
Give us this day our daily bread;
and forgive us our trespasses,
as we forgive those who trespass against us;
and lead us not into temptation,
but deliver us from evil.

"If you forgive men their transgressions, your heavenly Father will forgive you. But if you do not forgive men, neither will your Father forgive your transgressions."

Friends, today's Gospel gives us the Our Father. It asks that God's will be done "on earth as it is in heaven," but biblical cosmology sees these two realms as interpenetrating fields of force. Heaven, the arena of God and the angels, touches upon and calls out to earth, the arena of humans, animals, plants, and planets.

Salvation, therefore, is a matter of the meeting of heaven and earth, so that God might reign as thoroughly here below as he does on high. Jesus' great prayer, which is constantly on the lips of Christians, is distinctively Jewish in inspiration: "Thy Kingdom come, thy will be done, on earth as it is in heaven."

This is decidedly not a prayer that we might escape from the earth, but rather that earth and heaven might come together. The Lord's Prayer raises to a new level what the prophet Isaiah anticipated: "The earth shall be filled with knowledge of the Lord, as water covers the sea."

The first Christians saw the Resurrection of Jesus as the commencement of the process by which earth and heaven were being reconciled. They appreciated the risen Christ as the one who would bring the justice of heaven to this world.

REFLECT: What does it mean to "hold God's name holy above all" in your own life? Is anything competing for that top position of honor?

Wednesday, February 24, 2021

First Week of Lent

While still more people gathered in the crowd, Jesus said to them, "This generation is an evil generation; it seeks a sign, but no sign will be given it, except the sign of Jonah. Just as Jonah became a sign to the Ninevites, so will the Son of Man be to this generation. At the judgment the queen of the south will rise with the men of this generation and she will condemn them, because she came from the ends of the earth to hear the wisdom of Solomon, and there is something greater than Solomon here. At the judgment the men of Nineveh will arise with this generation and condemn it, because at the preaching of Jonah they repented, and there is something greater than Jonah here."

LENTEN *GOSPEL* REFLECTIONS

Friends, in today's Gospel, Jesus tells the crowds who seek a sign that they will only receive the sign of Jonah: "Just as Jonah became a sign to the Ninevites, so will the Son of Man be to this generation."

Jonah is called by God to preach to Nineveh, which is described as an enormously large city. It takes, they say, three days to walk through it. I can't help but think of Nineveh as one of our large, modern cities, a center of all sorts of worldly activity and preoccupation.

What would its conversion look like? A turning back to God as the only enduring good. After hearing the word of Jonah, the Ninevites proclaim a fast, and all of them, great and small, put on sackcloth. What is the purpose of these ascetic practices? To wean people away from an attachment to worldly pleasures.

Go beyond the mind that you have. Repent. Live as though nothing in this world finally matters. And you will be living in the kingdom of God!

REFLECT: In what areas of your life do you need to "turn back to God"? How will you start this process now?

_____

_____

_____

_____

_____

_____

_____

_____

_____

Thursday, February 25, 2021

First Week of Lent

MATTHEW 7:7-12

Jesus said to his disciples: "Ask and it will be given to you; seek and you will find; knock and the door will be opened to you. For everyone who asks, receives; and the one who seeks, finds; and to the one who knocks, the door will be opened. Which one of you would hand his son a stone when he asked for a loaf of bread, or a snake when he asked for a fish? If you then, who are wicked, know how to give good gifts to your children, how much more will your heavenly Father give good things to those who ask him.

"Do to others whatever you would have them do to you. This is the law and the prophets."

Friends, today's Gospel urges us to persist in prayer. The Lord wants us to ask with persistence, even stubbornness.

Now, we must not think of God as becoming exasperated by our prayer of petition, but the clear implication is that we will get what we want through persistence: "Ask and it will be given to you; seek and you will find; knock and the door will be opened to you."

How do we make sense of this? For me, the best explanation is offered by St. Augustine. He said that God doesn't always give us immediately what we ask for, and in fact, he compels us to ask again and again. The Lord wants to stretch us, expanding our desire so as to receive the gift he desires to give us.

If we got everything we wanted, right away and without effort, we wouldn't appreciate what we've received, and we wouldn't really be capable of taking it in. It would be like pouring new wine into old, shrunken wineskins, resulting in a loss of both the skins and the wine.

So if the gift doesn't come right away, don't despair; rather, feel your very soul expanding in anticipation.

REFLECT: Think of something you prayed about repeatedly for a very long time. When your prayer was answered, how had you changed from start to finish?

_____

_____

_____

_____

_____

_____

_____

Friday, February 26, 2021

First Week of Lent

MATTHEW 5:20-26

Jesus said to his disciples: "I tell you, unless your righteousness surpasses that of the scribes and Pharisees, you will not enter into the Kingdom of heaven.

"You have heard that it was said to your ancestors, *You shall not kill; and whoever kills will be liable to judgment.* But I say to you, whoever is angry with his brother will be liable to judgment, and whoever says to his brother, Raqa, will be answerable to the Sanhedrin, and whoever says, 'You fool,' will be liable to fiery Gehenna. Therefore, if you bring your gift to the altar, and there recall that your brother has anything against you, leave your gift there at the altar, go first and be reconciled with your brother, and then come and offer your gift. Settle with your opponent quickly while on the way to court. Otherwise your opponent will hand you over to the judge, and the judge will hand you over to the guard, and you will be thrown into prison. Amen, I say to you, you will not be released until you have paid the last penny."

Friends, in today's Gospel, Jesus teaches that if a brother has something against us, we must be reconciled with him before we offer our gift at the altar. This reconciling requires a change of heart and mind.

The word often misleadingly translated as "repent" is *metanoiete*. This Greek term is based upon two words, *meta* (beyond) and *nous* (mind or spirit), and thus, in its most basic form, it means something like "go beyond the mind that you have."

The English word "repent" has a moralizing overtone, suggesting a change in behavior or action, whereas Jesus' term seems to be hinting at a change at a far more fundamental level of one's being. Jesus urges his listeners to change their way of knowing, their way of perceiving and grasping reality, their mode of seeing.

What Jesus implies is this: a new state of affairs has arrived, the divine and human have met, but the way you customarily see is going to blind you to this novelty. Minds, eyes, ears, senses, perceptions—all have to be opened up, turned around, revitalized. *Metanoia*, mind transformation, is Jesus' first recommendation.

REFLECT: What does the fact that the divine and the human have met and are forever joined in the person of Jesus Christ indicate about God's reality, which is often beyond what our five senses perceive?

Saturday, February 27, 2021

First Week of Lent

MATTHEW 5:43-48

Jesus said to his disciples: "You have heard that it was said, *You shall love your neighbor and hate your enemy.* But I say to you, love your enemies, and pray for those who persecute you, that you may be children of your heavenly Father, for he makes his sun rise on the bad and the good, and causes rain to fall on the just and the unjust. For if you love those who love you, what recompense will you have? Do not the tax collectors do the same? And if you greet your brothers and sisters only, what is unusual about that? Do not the pagans do the same? So be perfect, just as your heavenly Father is perfect."

Friends, today, in the Sermon on the Mount, the Lord commands us to love our enemies.

What is the test of love? Jesus couldn't be clearer in the discourse he delivers the night before he died. "No one has greater love than this, to lay down one's life for one's friends." If love is willing the good of the other as other, this has to be the fullest expression, the final word, of love.

There is another way to test love: the love of enemies, those who cannot or will not pay you back. This also takes place in the cross of Jesus. Jews, Romans, Pharisees, Sadducees, his own disciples—everyone betrays him, runs from him, denies him, actively arranges for his death. And yet these are the very people that he loves, the very people for whom he gives his life.

The final test is what Jesus does when he returns from the dead. To the very people that contributed to his demise he says, "Shalom." This is how we are loved; this is how we must love. Everything else is commentary.

REFLECT: Name an enemy or someone you intensely dislike. What is it about them that bothers you? How do these feelings shed light on your own weaknesses?

_____

_____

_____

_____

_____

_____

_____

_____

_____

Sunday, February 28, 2021

Second Sunday of Lent

MARK 9:2-10

Jesus took Peter, James, and John and led them up a high mountain apart by themselves. And he was transfigured before them, and his clothes became dazzling white, such as no fuller on earth could bleach them. Then Elijah appeared to them along with Moses, and they were conversing with Jesus. Then Peter said to Jesus in reply, "Rabbi, it is good that we are here! Let us make three tents: one for you, one for Moses, and one for Elijah." He hardly knew what to say, they were so terrified. Then a cloud came, casting a shadow over them; from the cloud came a voice, "This is my beloved Son. Listen to him." Suddenly, looking around, they no longer saw anyone but Jesus alone with them.

As they were coming down from the mountain, he charged them not to relate what they had seen to anyone, except when the Son of Man had risen from the dead. So they kept the matter to themselves, questioning what rising from the dead meant.

Friends, today's Gospel presents the Transfiguration of Christ. What is the Transfiguration itself? Mark speaks literally of a metamorphosis, a going beyond the form that he had. If I can use Paul's language, it is "the knowledge of the glory of God on the face of Jesus Christ." In and through his humble humanity, his divinity shines forth. The proximity of his divinity in no way compromises the integrity of his humanity, but rather makes it shine in greater beauty. This is the New Testament version of the burning bush.

The Jesus who is both divine and human is the Jesus who is evangelically compelling. If he is only divine, then he doesn't touch us; if he is only human, he can't save us. His splendor consists in the coming together of the two natures, without mixing, mingling, or confusion.

This same Jesus then accompanies his disciples back down the mountain and walks with them in the ordinary rhythms of their lives. This is the Christ who wants to reign as Lord of our lives in every detail. If we forget about this dimension, then Jesus becomes a distant memory, a figure from the past.

REFLECT: How does the reality of the Transfiguration and the Resurrection give you hope?

_____

_____

_____

_____

Monday, March 1, 2021

Second Week of Lent

LUKE 6:36-38

J esus said to his disciples:
"Be merciful, just as your Father is merciful.

"Stop judging and you will not be judged. Stop condemning and you will not be condemned. Forgive and you will be forgiven. Give and gifts will be given to you; a good measure, packed together, shaken down, and overflowing, will be poured into your lap. For the measure with which you measure will in return be measured out to you."

Friends, in today's Gospel, Jesus calls us to "be merciful, just as your Father is merciful."

Mercy or tender compassion (*chesed* in the Hebrew of the Old Testament) is God's most distinctive characteristic. St. Augustine reminded us that we are, by our very nature, ordered to God. But since God is tender mercy, "having" God is tantamount to exercising compassion, being merciful ourselves.

And attend to what Jesus says next: "Stop judging and you will not be judged. Stop condemning and you will not be condemned.

Forgive and you will be forgiven. Give and gifts will be given to you." According to the "physics" of the spiritual order, the more one draws on the divine life, the more one receives that life, precisely because it *is* a gift and is properly infinite. God's life is had, as it were, on the fly: when you receive it as a gift, you must give it away, since it only exists in gift form, and then you will find more of it flooding into your heart.

If you want to be happy, Jesus is saying, this divine love, this *chesed* of God, must be central to your life; it must be your beginning, your middle, and your end.

REFLECT: Jesus seems to be intensifying the Golden Rule to mean, "Do unto others as you would have God do unto you." How does this upgraded Golden Rule reflect God's mercy?

_____

_____

_____

_____

_____

_____

_____

_____

_____

Tuesday, March 2, 2021

Second Week of Lent

MATTHEW 23:1-12

Jesus spoke to the crowds and to his disciples, saying, "The scribes and the Pharisees have taken their seat on the chair of Moses. Therefore, do and observe all things whatsoever they tell you, but do not follow their example. For they preach but they do not practice. They tie up heavy burdens hard to carry and lay them on people's shoulders, but they will not lift a finger to move them. All their works are performed to be seen. They widen their phylacteries and lengthen their tassels. They love places of honor at banquets, seats of honor in synagogues, greetings in marketplaces, and the salutation 'Rabbi.' As for you, do not be called 'Rabbi.' You have but one teacher, and you are all brothers. Call no one on earth your father; you have but one Father in heaven. Do not be called 'Master'; you have but one master, the Christ. The greatest among you must be your servant. Whoever exalts himself will be humbled; but whoever humbles himself will be exalted."

LENTEN *GOSPEL* REFLECTIONS

Friends, our Gospel for today focuses on the pitfalls and ideals of religious leadership. This is a week when priests, ministers, and preachers have to preach to themselves. Jesus turns his sharp eye and withering critique on the many ways that religious leaders fall into corruption.

It is hard to miss the practical application of these texts to our troubled time, a period when clerical corruption and misconduct has been vividly on display. Jesus makes a distinction of capital importance. "The scribes and Pharisees have taken their seat on the chair of Moses. Therefore, do and observe all things whatsover they tell you." The Lord reminds us that they do sit legitimately in teaching offices and that their teaching should be, accordingly, respected.

In the fourth century, St. Augustine faced the challenge of the Donatists. They claimed that only pure and morally upright priests could legitimately dispense the sacraments. Augustine said, no, the personal evil of a minister does not compromise the validity of what he does sacramentally.

This principle is of great significance. Augustine, in imitation of Christ, says that there can be evil men who do and teach the works of God.

REFLECT: Why is it important that the validity of the sacraments does not depend upon the personal holiness of the minister?

_____

_____

_____

_____

Wednesday, March 3, 2021

Second Week of Lent

MATTHEW 20:17-28

As Jesus was going up to Jerusalem, he took the Twelve disciples aside by themselves, and said to them on the way, "Behold, we are going up to Jerusalem, and the Son of Man will be handed over to the chief priests and the scribes, and they will condemn him to death, and hand him over to the Gentiles to be mocked and scourged and crucified, and he will be raised on the third day."

Then the mother of the sons of Zebedee approached Jesus with her sons and did him homage, wishing to ask him for something. He said to her, "What do you wish?" She answered him, "Command that these two sons of mine sit, one at your right and the other at your left, in your kingdom." Jesus said in reply, "You do not know what you are asking. Can you drink the chalice that I am going to drink?" They said to him, "We can." He replied, "My chalice you will indeed drink, but to sit at my right and at my left, this is not mine to give but is for those for whom it has been prepared by my Father." When the ten heard this, they became indignant at the two brothers. But Jesus summoned them and said,

> "You know that the rulers of the Gentiles lord it over them, and the great ones make their authority over them felt. But it shall not be so among you. Rather, whoever wishes to be great among you shall be your servant; whoever wishes to be first among you shall be your slave. Just so, the Son of Man did not come to be served but to serve and to give his life as a ransom for many."

Friends, today in our Gospel the mother of James and John asks Jesus on their behalf for high places of authority in his kingdom. Ah, there is the voice of ambition. Some people don't care at all about money or power or pleasure—but they care passionately about honor. A lot of people can identify with James and John. They want to go places, they want to be movers and shakers in society. Perhaps a number of people reading this reflection are filled with these emotions.

But Jesus turns the tables on them: "You do not know what you are asking." He is indeed a King, and he will indeed rule Israel, but his crown will be made of thorns, and his throne will be a Roman instrument of torture.

And so he tries to clarify: "Can you drink the chalice that I am going to drink?" The key to honor in the kingdom of God is to drink the cup of suffering, to be willing to suffer out of love, to give one's life away as a gift. Look at the lives of the saints. It is not about aggrandizing the ego, but emptying it out.

REFLECT: Are you drinking your cup of suffering alongside Jesus? If so, how do you think and feel about that suffering?

_____

_____

_____

_____

_____

_____

_____

_____

_____

_____

_____

_____

_____

_____

_____

_____

_____

Thursday, March 4, 2021

Second Week of Lent

Jesus said to the Pharisees: "There was a rich man who dressed in purple garments and fine linen and dined sumptuously each day. And lying at his door was a poor man named Lazarus, covered with sores, who would gladly have eaten his fill of the scraps that fell from the rich man's table. Dogs even used to come and lick his sores. When the poor man died, he was carried away by angels to the bosom of Abraham. The rich man also died and was buried, and from the netherworld, where he was in torment, he raised his eyes and saw Abraham far off and Lazarus at his side. And he cried out, 'Father Abraham, have pity on me. Send Lazarus to dip the tip of his finger in water and cool my tongue, for I am suffering torment in these flames.' Abraham replied, 'My child, remember that you received what was good during your lifetime while Lazarus likewise received what was bad; but now he is comforted here, whereas you are tormented. Moreover, between us and you a great chasm is established to prevent anyone from crossing who might wish to go from our side to yours or from your side to ours.' He said, 'Then I beg you, father, send him to my father's house, for I have five brothers, so that he may warn them, lest they too come to this place of torment.' But Abraham replied, 'They have Moses and the prophets. Let them listen to them.' He said, 'Oh no, father Abraham, but if someone from the dead goes to them, they will repent.' Then Abraham said, 'If they will not listen to Moses and the prophets, neither will they be persuaded if someone should rise from the dead.'"

Friends, today's Gospel tells the story of the rich man and the poor man, Lazarus, at his gate.

God is not pleased with this kind of economic inequality, and he burns with passion to set things right. Even though it makes us uncomfortable—and God knows it does, especially those of us who live in the most affluent society in the world—we can't avoid it because it's everywhere in the Bible.

St. Thomas Aquinas says, "We must distinguish between ownership and the use of property." We have a right to ownership, through our hard work or inheritance. Fair enough. But with regard to the use of those things, then, says Thomas, we must always be concerned for the common good and not our own.

That's an extraordinarily powerful claim, though it's stated in rather sober language. Yes, you have a right to property, to ownership, but when and how you use what you own, that is always a matter of the common good, which especially includes Lazarus at your gate: whoever is suffering and in need.

REFLECT: Make a list of how you use your property for the common good. Try to add to that list before Easter.

_____

_____

_____

_____

_____

_____

_____

_____

_____

_____

_____

_____

Friday, March 5, 2021

Second Week of Lent

MATTHEW 21:33-43,45-46

Jesus said to the chief priests and the elders of the people: "Hear another parable. There was a landowner who planted a vineyard, put a hedge around it, dug a wine press in it, and built a tower. Then he leased it to tenants and went on a journey. When vintage time drew near, he sent his servants to the tenants to obtain his produce. But the tenants seized the servants and one they beat, another they killed, and a third they stoned. Again he sent other servants, more numerous than the first ones, but they treated them in the same way. Finally, he sent his son to them, thinking, 'They will respect my son.' But when the tenants saw the son, they said to one another, 'This is the heir. Come, let us kill him and acquire his inheritance.' They seized him, threw him out of the vineyard, and killed him. What will the owner of the vineyard do to those tenants when he comes?" They answered him, He will put those wretched men to a wretched death and lease his vineyard to other tenants who will give him the produce at the proper times." Jesus said to them, "Did you never read in the Scriptures:

*'The stone that the builders rejected
has become the cornerstone;*

> *by the Lord has this been done,*
> *and it is wonderful in our eyes'?*
>
> Therefore, I say to you, the Kingdom of God will
> be taken away from you and given to a people that
> will produce its fruit." When the chief priests and
> the Pharisees heard his parables, they knew that he
> was speaking about them. And although they were
> attempting to arrest him, they feared the crowds, for
> they regarded him as a prophet.

Friends, just before his Passion and death, Jesus tells the striking
story that is our Gospel for today. The fertile vineyard stands for
Israel, his chosen people. But it could be broadened out to include
the world. What do we learn from this beautiful image? That
God has made for his people a place where they can find rest,
enjoyment, good work.

We—Israel, the Church, the world—are not the owners of this
vineyard; we are tenants. One of the most fundamental spiritual
mistakes we can make is to think that we own the world. We
are tenants, entrusted with the responsibility of caring for it, but
everything that we have and are is on loan. Our lives are not
about us.

Christ is God's judgment. We are all under his judgment. In
the measure that we reject him or refuse to listen to him, we

place our tenancy in jeopardy. And so the great question that arises from this reading: How am I using the gifts that God gave me for God's purposes? My money? My time? My talents? My creativity? My relationships? All is for God, and thus all is under God's judgment.

REFLECT: How are you using the gifts that God gave you for God's purposes?

_____

_____

_____

_____

_____

_____

_____

_____

_____

_____

_____

_____

_____

Saturday, March 6, 2021

Second Week of Lent

LUKE 15:1-3,11-32

Tax collectors and sinners were all drawing near to listen to Jesus, but the Pharisees and scribes began to complain, saying, "This man welcomes sinners and eats with them." So to them Jesus addressed this parable. "A man had two sons, and the younger son said to his father, 'Father, give me the share of your estate that should come to me.' So the father divided the property between them. After a few days, the younger son collected all his belongings and set off to a distant country where he squandered his inheritance on a life of dissipation. When he had freely spent everything, a severe famine struck that country, and he found himself in dire need. So he hired himself out to one of the local citizens who sent him to his farm to tend the swine. And he longed to eat his fill of the pods on which the swine fed, but nobody gave him any. Coming to his senses he thought, 'How many of my father's hired workers have more than enough food to eat, but here am I, dying from hunger. I shall get up and go to my father and I shall say to him, "Father, I have sinned against heaven and against you. I no longer deserve to be called your son; treat me as you would treat one of your hired workers."' So he got up and went back to his father. While he was still a long way off, his father caught sight of him, and was filled with compassion. He ran to his son, embraced him and kissed him. His son said to him, 'Father, I have sinned against heaven and against you; I no longer deserve to be called your son.' But his father ordered his servants, 'Quickly, bring the finest robe and put it on him; put a ring on his finger and sandals on his feet. Take the fattened calf and slaughter it. Then let us celebrate with a feast, because this son of mine was dead, and has come to life again; he was lost, and has been found.' Then the celebration began. Now the older son had been out in the field and, on his way back, as he neared the house, he heard the sound of music and dancing. He called one of the servants and asked what this might mean. The servant said to him, 'Your brother has returned and your father has slaughtered the fattened calf because he has him back safe and sound.' He became angry, and when he refused to enter the house, his father came out and pleaded with him. He said to his father in reply, 'Look, all these years I served you and not once did I disobey your orders; yet you never gave me even a young goat to feast on with my friends. But when your son returns who swallowed up your property with prostitutes, for him you slaughter the fattened calf.' He said to him, 'My son, you are here with me

always; everything I have is yours. But now we must
celebrate and rejoice, because your brother was dead
and has come to life again; he was lost and has been
found.'"

Friends, our Gospel today is Jesus' best-known parable: the story
of the prodigal son.

In considering this narrative, we are dealing with an icon of the
Father told by the one who is himself the Icon of the Father.
Thus we have Jesus indirectly crafting a subtle self-portrait. The
gathering embrace of the father in the story mirrors that of the
heavenly Father, which in turn is represented in that of Jesus.

What happens when the father embraces his son and kisses
him? The boy speaks: "Father, I have sinned against heaven and
against you. I no longer deserve to be called your son." Whenever
characters in the Bible come close to the divine grace, they
experience a heightened sense of their own unworthiness. This is
the dynamic at work in the case of the prodigal son.

But his father ignores his carefully rehearsed speech, and with
an eagerness bordering on impatience, instructs his servants to
prepare a celebration. Our participation in the flow of the divine
life is, necessarily, a gift. It cannot, in principle, be earned or
merited, but only accepted. We can only be embraced by it.

REFLECT: Do you believe you can earn a place in God's kingdom? Why or why not?

_____

_____

_____

_____

_____

_____

_____

_____

_____

_____

_____

_____

_____

_____

_____

_____

Sunday, March 7, 2021

Third Sunday of Lent

Since the Passover of the Jews was near, Jesus went up to Jerusalem. He found in the temple area those who sold oxen, sheep, and doves, as well as the money changers seated there. He made a whip out of cords and drove them all out of the temple area, with the sheep and oxen, and spilled the coins of the money changers and overturned their tables, and to those who sold doves he said, "Take these out of here, and stop making my Father's house a marketplace." His disciples recalled the words of Scripture, *Zeal for your house will consume me.* At this the Jews answered and said to him, "What sign can you show us for doing this?" Jesus answered and said to them, "Destroy this temple and in three days I will raise it up." The Jews said, "This temple has been under construction for forty-six years, and you will raise it up in three days?" But he was speaking about the temple of his body. Therefore, when he was raised from the dead, his disciples remembered that he had said this, and they came to believe the Scripture and the word Jesus had spoken.

While he was in Jerusalem for the feast of Passover, many began to believe in his name when they saw the signs he was doing. But Jesus would not trust himself to them because he knew them all, and did not need anyone to testify about human nature. He himself understood it well.

Friend, today we read an episode recorded in all four Gospels—namely, Jesus' paradigmatically prophetic act of cleansing the temple.

Jesus is prophetic to the depth of his being, and his prophetic vocation will manifest itself in all of his speech, gestures, and actions. This entails that his confrontation with fallen powers and dysfunctional traditions will be highly focused, intense, and disruptive.

Standing at the heart of the holy city of Jerusalem, the temple was the political, economic, cultural, and religious center of the nation. Turning over the tables of the money-changers and driving out the merchants, shouting in high dudgeon, upsetting the order of that place was to strike at the most sacred institution of the culture, the unassailable embodiment of the tradition. It was to show oneself as critic in the most radical and surprising sense possible. That this act of Jesus the warrior flowed from the depth of his prophetic identity is witnessed to by the author of John's Gospel: "His disciples recalled the words of scripture, *Zeal for you house will consume me.*"

Many of the historical critics of the New Testament hold that this event—shocking, unprecedented, perverse—is what finally persuaded the leaders that Jesus merited execution.

REFLECT: Have you ever had to confront "fallen powers and dysfunctional traditions" as Jesus did in the temple? What happened and how did you respond?

_____

_____

_____

_____

_____

_____

_____

_____

Monday, March 8, 2021

Third Week of Lent

LUKE 4:24-30

Jesus said to the people in the synagogue at Nazareth: "Amen, I say to you, no prophet is accepted in his own native place. Indeed, I tell you, there were many widows in Israel in the days of Elijah when the sky was closed for three and a half years and a severe famine spread over the entire land. It was to none of these that Elijah was sent, but only to a widow in Zarephath in the land of Sidon. Again, there were many lepers in Israel during the time of Elisha the prophet; yet not one of them was cleansed, but only Naaman the Syrian." When the people in the synagogue heard this, they were all filled with fury. They rose up, drove him out of the town, and led him to the brow of the hill on which their town had been built, to hurl him down headlong. But he passed through the midst of them and went away.

LENTEN *GOSPEL* REFLECTIONS

Friends, today's Gospel develops a theme that is uncomfortable. It tells how the people of Nazareth rejected Jesus. Authentically religious people, authentically spiritual people, will almost always be opposed. The logic behind this is simple and unanswerable:

we live in a world gone wrong, a world turned upside down; therefore, when someone comes speaking the truth to us, we will think that they are crazy and dangerous.

Think for just a moment what would happen to you if you consistently and publicly spoke the word of God to our culture. If you spoke out against abortion, euthanasia, human trafficking, rampant materialism, and ideological secularism, what would happen to you? If you presented, in a full-throated way, the full range of Catholic social and moral and spiritual teaching, what would they do to you? Trust me, they would throw you in a version of Jeremiah's cistern.

REFLECT: How can you confront your fear and take a step toward speaking the word of God to the culture as Jesus did in his time?

_____

_____

_____

_____

_____

_____

_____

_____

_____

Tuesday, March 9, 2021

Third Week of Lent

MATTHEW 18:21-35

Peter approached Jesus and asked him, "Lord, if my brother sins against me, how often must I forgive him? As many as seven times?" Jesus answered, "I say to you, not seven times but seventy-seven times. That is why the Kingdom of heaven may be likened to a king who decided to settle accounts with his servants. When he began the accounting, a debtor was brought before him who owed him a huge amount. Since he had no way of paying it back, his master ordered him to be sold, along with his wife, his children, and all his property, in payment of the debt. At that, the servant fell down, did him homage, and said, 'Be patient with me, and I will pay you back in full.' Moved with compassion the master of that servant let him go and forgave him the loan. When that servant had left, he found one of his fellow servants who owed him a much smaller amount. He seized him and started to choke him, demanding, 'Pay back what you owe.' Falling to his knees, his fellow servant begged him, 'Be patient with me, and I will pay you back.' But he refused. Instead, he had him put in prison until he paid back the debt. Now when his fellow servants saw what had happened, they were deeply disturbed, and went to their master and reported the whole affair. His master summoned him and said to him, 'You wicked servant! I forgave you your entire debt because you begged me to. Should you not have had pity on your fellow servant, as I had pity on you?' Then in anger his master handed him over to the torturers until he should pay back the whole debt. So will my heavenly Father do to you, unless each of you forgives your brother from your heart."

Friends, today's Gospel gives us the parable of the unforgiving servant, which reveals what is at the root of our inability to forgive.

In the deepest sense, we don't belong to ourselves. Everything we have and all that we are comes from God. We are meant, with all of our gifts, to serve God's purposes. Our very existence comes from God, but so does the forgiveness of our sins. Through no merit of ours, Christ has died for our sins and offered us the divine mercy. The upshot is this: there is nothing particularly stable about the self, nothing that it can claim for its own. All that it has is received as a gift.

Well, the incapacity to forgive comes from one place: a false sense of the substantial self. If my life belongs to me, then I will cling to resentment, anger, and self-righteousness when my dignity has been compromised. But when we realize that our life is not about us—when we put our forgiveness of others in relation to God's forgiveness of us—then we find that real forgiveness is possible.

REFLECT: Think of the last time you had difficulty forgiving someone. How did your sense of your own "substantial self" make you hesitant to forgive?

_____

_____

_____

_____

_____

_____

_____

_____

_____

_____

_____

_____

_____

Wednesday, March 10, 2021

Third Week of Lent

MATTHEW 5:17-19

Jesus said to his disciples: "Do not think that I have come to abolish the law or the prophets. I have come not to abolish but to fulfill. Amen, I say to you, until heaven and earth pass away, not the smallest letter or the smallest part of a letter will pass from the law, until all things have taken place. Therefore, whoever breaks one of the least of these commandments and teaches others to do so will be called least in the Kingdom of heaven. But whoever obeys and teaches these commandments will be called greatest in the Kingdom of heaven."

Friends, in today's Gospel, Jesus promises that he has not come to abolish the Law but to fulfill it. Matthew says that Jesus went up a mountain, sat down, and commenced to teach, calling to mind Moses, who went up Mount Sinai to receive the Ten Commandments from God.

Therefore, Jesus is being presented here as the new Moses who will promulgate from this Galilean mountain the definitive Law. I realize that this immediately poses a problem for contemporary readers, who are put off by a religion that leads with laws, rules, and prohibitions. An Irish wag once summed up the Catholicism that he was taught with this phrase: "In the beginning was the word, and the word was no!"

Since the Ten Commandments have been honored mostly in the breach, why should anyone think it a good idea to introduce new and even more stringent laws? But then we attend to the first word out of the mouth of the lawgiver: "Blessed," "Happy." The law that the New Moses offers is a pattern of life that promises to make us happy.

REFLECT: Jesus tells us how to be happy when he shares the Beatitudes. How can laws or rules play a role in making us happy?

_____

_____

_____

_____

_____

_____

_____

_____

_____

Thursday, March 11, 2021

Third Week of Lent

LUKE 11:14-23

Jesus was driving out a demon that was mute, and when the demon had gone out, the mute man spoke and the crowds were amazed. Some of them said, "By the power of Beelzebul, the prince of demons, he drives out demons." Others, to test him, asked him for a sign from heaven. But he knew their thoughts and said to them, "Every kingdom divided against itself will be laid waste and house will fall against house. And if Satan is divided against himself, how will his kingdom stand? For you say that it is by Beelzebul that I drive out demons. If I, then, drive out demons by Beelzebul, by whom do your own people drive them out? Therefore they will be your judges. But if it is by the finger of God that I drive out demons, then the Kingdom of God has come upon you. When a strong man fully armed guards his palace, his possessions are safe. But when one stronger than he attacks and overcomes him, he takes away the armor on which he relied and distributes the spoils. Whoever is not with me is against me, and whoever does not gather with me scatters."

Friends, in today's Gospel, we learn of a person possessed by a demon. Jesus meets the man and drives out the demon, but then he is immediately accused of being in league with Satan. Some of the witnesses said, "By the power of Beelzebul, the prince of demons, he drives out demons."

Jesus' response is wonderful in its logic and laconicism: "Every kingdom divided against itself will be laid waste and house will fall against house. And if Satan is divided against himself, how will his kingdom stand?"

The demonic power is always one of scattering. It breaks up communion. But Jesus, as always, is the voice of *communio*, of one bringing things back together.

Think back to Jesus' feeding of the five thousand. Facing a large, hungry crowd, his disciples beg him to "dismiss the crowds so that they can go to the villages and buy food for themselves." But Jesus answers, "There is no need for them to go away; give them some food yourselves."

Whatever drives the Church apart is an echo of this "dismiss the crowds" impulse, and a reminder of the demonic tendency to divide. In times of trial and threat, this is a very common instinct. We blame, attack, break up, and disperse. But Jesus is right: "There is no need for them to go away."

REFLECT: What do you see in the Catholic Church today that is a source of division? What do you see that is a source of communion? How can you be an agent of communion in your own parish?

Friday, March 12, 2021

Third Week of Lent

MARK 12:28-34

One of the scribes came to Jesus and asked him, "Which is the first of all the commandments?" Jesus replied, "The first is this: *Hear, O Israel! The Lord our God is Lord alone! You shall love the Lord your God with all your heart, with all your soul, with all your mind, and with all your strength.* The second is this: *You shall love your neighbor as yourself.* There is no other commandment greater than these." The scribe said to him, "Well said, teacher. You are right in saying, *He is One and there is no other than he.* And *to love him with all your heart, with all your understanding, with all your strength, and to love your neighbor as yourself* is worth more than all burnt offerings and sacrifices." And when Jesus saw that he answered with understanding, he said to him, "You are not far from the Kingdom of God." And no one dared to ask him any more questions.

Friends, in today's Gospel, the Lord says that the second greatest commandment is to love your neighbor as yourself.

Love is not primarily a feeling or an instinct; rather, it is the act of willing the good of the other as other. It is radical self-gift, living for the sake of the other. To be kind to someone so that he might be kind to you, or to treat a fellow human being justly so that he, in turn, might treat you with justice, is not to love, for such moves are tantamount to indirect self-interest.

Truly to love is to move outside of the black hole of one's egotism, to resist the centripetal force that compels one to assume the attitude of self-protection. But this means that love is rightly described as a "theological virtue," for it represents a participation in the love that God is.

Since God has no needs, only God can utterly exist for the sake of the other. All of the great masters of the Christian spiritual tradition saw that we are able to love only inasmuch as we have received, as a grace, a share in the very life, energy, and nature of God.

REFLECT: Examine how you love others, searching out any move to indirect self-interest that may exist. How can you make sure your love "wills the good of the other"?

_____

_____

_____

_____

_____

_____

_____

Saturday, March 13, 2021
Third Week of Lent

LUKE 18:9-14

Jesus addressed this parable to those who were convinced of their own righteousness and despised everyone else. "Two people went up to the temple area to pray; one was a Pharisee and the other was a tax collector. The Pharisee took up his position and spoke this prayer to himself, 'O God, I thank you that I am not like the rest of humanity—greedy, dishonest, adulterous—or even like this tax collector. I fast twice a week, and I pay tithes on my whole income.' But the tax collector stood off at a distance and would not even raise his eyes to heaven but beat his breast and prayed, 'O God, be merciful to me a sinner.' I tell you, the latter went home justified, not the former; for everyone who exalts himself will be humbled, and the one who humbles himself will be exalted."

Friends, today Jesus tells us of the Pharisee and the tax collector—so, stereotypically righteous and unrighteous people—who both enter the temple to pray. But what a world of difference in their manner of praying!

The entire point of religion is to make us humble before God and to open us to the path of love. Everything else is more or less a footnote. Liturgy, prayer, the precepts of the Church, the Commandments, sacraments, sacramentals—all of it—are finally meant to conform us to the way of love. When they instead turn us away from that path, they have been undermined.

Both St. Paul and the Gospel writers—as well as Jesus himself, of course—are intensely aware of this danger. This is precisely why Paul speaks of the dangers of the Law. He knew that people often use the Law as a weapon of aggression: since I know what is right and wrong in some detail, then I am uniquely positioned to point out your flaws. And when I point out your flaws, I elevate myself. In short, the Law, which is a gift from God, has been co-opted for the purposes of the ego.

REFLECT: How can you incorporate the prayer of the tax collector into your own spiritual life?

_____

_____

_____

_____

_____

_____

_____

Sunday, March 14, 2021

Fourth Sunday of Lent

JOHN 3:14-21

Jesus said to Nicodemus:
"Just as Moses lifted up the serpent in the desert,
so must the Son of Man be lifted up, so that
everyone who believes in him may have eternal life."

For God so loved the world that he gave his only
Son, so that everyone who believes in him might not
perish but might have eternal life. For God did not
send his Son into the world to condemn the world,
but that the world might be saved through him.
Whoever believes in him will not be condemned,
but whoever does not believe has already been
condemned, because he has not believed in the
name of the only Son of God. And this is the
verdict, that the light came into the world,
but people preferred darkness to light, because their
works were evil. For everyone who does wicked
things hates the light and does not come toward the
light, so that his works might not be exposed.
But whoever lives the truth comes to the light, so
that his works may be clearly seen as done in God.

Friends, our Gospel today includes one of the best-known passages of Scripture: "God so loved the world that he gave his only Son, so that everyone who believes in him might not perish but might have eternal life."

In his passion to set right a disjointed universe, God broke open his own heart in love. The Father sent, not simply a representative, spokesman, or plenipotentiary, but his own Son into the dysfunction of the world so that he might gather that world into the bliss of the divine life. God's center—the love between the Father and the Son—is now offered as our center; God's heart breaks open so as to include even the worst and most hopeless among us.

In so many spiritual traditions, the emphasis is placed on the human quest for God, but this is reversed in Christianity. Christians do not believe that God is dumbly "out there," like a mountain waiting to be climbed by various religious searchers. On the contrary, God, like the hound of heaven in Francis Thompson's poem, comes relentlessly searching after us. Because of this questing and self-emptying divine love, we become friends of God, sharers in the communion of the Trinity.

REFLECT: How is the Christian way of seeing different from the culture's way of seeing?

_____

_____

_____

Monday, March 15, 2021

Fourth Week of Lent

JOHN 4:43-54

At that time Jesus left [Samaria] for Galilee. For Jesus himself testified that a prophet has no honor in his native place. When he came into Galilee, the Galileans welcomed him, since they had seen all he had done in Jerusalem at the feast; for they themselves had gone to the feast.

Then he returned to Cana in Galilee, where he had made the water wine. Now there was a royal official whose son was ill in Capernaum. When he heard that Jesus had arrived in Galilee from Judea, he went to him and asked him to come down and heal his son, who was near death. Jesus said to him, "Unless you people see signs and wonders, you will not believe." The royal official said to him, "Sir, come down before my child dies." Jesus said to him, "You may go; your son will live." The man believed what Jesus said to him and left. While the man was on his way back, his slaves met him and told him that his boy would live. He asked them when he began to recover. They told him, "The fever left him

> yesterday, about one in the afternoon." The father
> realized that just at that time Jesus had said to him,
> "Your son will live," and he and his whole household
> came to believe. Now this was the second sign Jesus
> did when he came to Galilee from Judea.

Friends, our Gospel today tells of Jesus healing a royal official's son. The official asked him to heal his son, who was near death. Jesus said to him, "Unless you people see signs and wonders, you will not believe." But the royal official persisted. And Jesus told him his son would live. The man believed Jesus, and his son recovered.

Theologian Paul Tillich said that "faith" is the most misunderstood word in the religious vocabulary. And this is a tragedy, for faith stands at the very heart of the program; it is the *sine qua non* of the Christian thing. What is it? The opening line of Hebrews 11 has the right definition: "Faith is confident assurance concerning what we hope for, and conviction about things we do not see."

Faith is a straining ahead toward those things that are, at best, dimly glimpsed. But notice, please, that it is not a craven, hand-wringing, unsure business. It is "confident" and full of "conviction." Think of the great figures of faith, from Abraham to John Paul II: they are anything but shaky, indefinite, questioning people. Like the royal official, they are clear, focused, assured.

REFLECT: Contemplate your own level of faith. How does it exhibit "confident assurance concerning what we hope for, and conviction about things we do not see"?

_____

_____

_____

_____

_____

_____

_____

_____

_____

_____

_____

_____

_____

_____

_____

_____

_____

Tuesday, March 16, 2020

Fourth Week of Lent

There was a feast of the Jews, and Jesus went up to Jerusalem. Now there is in Jerusalem at the Sheep Gate a pool called in Hebrew Bethesda, with five porticoes. In these lay a large number of ill, blind, lame, and crippled. One man was there who had been ill for thirty eight years. When Jesus saw him lying there and knew that he had been ill for a long time, he said to him, "Do you want to be well?" The sick man answered him, "Sir, I have no one to put me into the pool when the water is stirred up; while I am on my way, someone else gets down there before me." Jesus said to him, "Rise, take up your mat, and walk." Immediately the man became well, took up his mat, and walked.

Now that day was a sabbath. So the Jews said to the man who was cured, "It is the sabbath, and it is not lawful for you to carry your mat." He answered them, "The man who made me well told me, 'Take up your mat and walk.'" They asked him, "Who is the man who told you, 'Take it up and walk'?" The man who was healed did not know who it was,

> for Jesus had slipped away, since there was a crowd
> there. After this Jesus found him in the temple area
> and said to him, "Look, you are well; do not sin any
> more, so that nothing worse may happen to you."
> The man went and told the Jews that Jesus was the
> one who had made him well. Therefore, the Jews
> began to persecute Jesus because he did this on a
> sabbath.

Friends, in today's Gospel, we find the beautiful healing of a paralyzed man who had been ill for thirty-eight years. Jesus sees the man lying on his mat, next to a pool, and asks, "Do you want to be well?" The man says yes, and Jesus replies, "Rise, take up your mat, and walk." Immediately, the man is healed.

Now, at this point, the story really heats up. We notice something that is frequently on display in the Gospels: the resistance to the creative work of God, the attempt to find any excuse, however lame, to deny it, to pretend it's not there, to condemn it.

One would expect that everyone around the cured man would rejoice, but just the contrary: the Jewish leaders are infuriated and confounded. They see the healed man and their first response is, "It is the Sabbath, and it is not lawful for you to carry your mat."

Why are they so reactive? Why don't they want this to be? We sinners don't like the ways of God. We find them troubling and threatening. Why? Because they undermine the games of oppression and exclusion that we rely upon in order to boost our own egos.

Let this encounter remind us that God's ways are not our ways, and that there is one even greater than the Sabbath.

REFLECT: When have the ways of God conflicted with your own ego (your plans, your will, your self)? What did you do?

_____

_____

_____

_____

_____

_____

_____

_____

_____

_____

_____

Wednesday, March 17, 2021

Fourth Week of Lent

JOHN 5:17-30

Jesus answered the Jews:
"My Father is at work until now, so I am at work."
For this reason they tried all the more to kill him,
because he not only broke the sabbath but he also
called God his own father, making himself equal to
God.

Jesus answered and said to them, "Amen, amen, I
say to you, the Son cannot do anything on his own,
but only what he sees the Father doing; for what he
does, the Son will do also. For the Father loves the
Son and shows him everything that he himself does,
and he will show him greater works than these,
so that you may be amazed. For just as the Father
raises the dead and gives life, so also does the Son
give life to whomever he wishes. Nor does the Father
judge anyone, but he has given all judgment to
the Son, so that all may honor the Son just as they
honor the Father. Whoever does not honor the Son
does not honor the Father who sent him. Amen,
amen, I say to you, whoever hears my word and
believes in the one who sent me has eternal life and
will not come to condemnation, but has passed
from death to life. Amen, amen, I say to you, the

hour is coming and is now here when the dead will hear the voice of the Son of God, and those who hear will live. For just as the Father has life in himself, so also he gave to the Son the possession of life in himself. And he gave him power to exercise judgment, because he is the Son of Man. Do not be amazed at this, because the hour is coming in which all who are in the tombs will hear his voice and will come out, those who have done good deeds to the resurrection of life, but those who have done wicked deeds to the resurrection of condemnation.

"I cannot do anything on my own; I judge as I hear, and my judgment is just, because I do not seek my own will but the will of the one who sent me."

Friends, in today's Gospel, we see Jesus as the judge who shows mercy and love. It is hard to read any two pages of the Bible—Old Testament or New—and not find the language of divine judgment.

Think of judgment as a sort of light, which reveals both the positive and the negative. Beautiful things look even more beautiful when the light shines on them; ugly things look even uglier when they come into the light. When the divine light shines, when judgment takes place, something like real love is unleashed.

Someone might avoid seeing the doctor for years, fearful that he will uncover something diseased or deadly. But how much better it is for you when you do, even when the doctor pronounces a harsh "judgment" on your physical condition!

And this is why judgment is the proper activity of a king. It is not the exercise of arbitrary power, but rather an exercise of real love.

REFLECT: What is revealed here about the identity of Jesus? Do you believe that Jesus is your Judge and your King? How does that affect the way you live?

_____

_____

_____

_____

_____

_____

_____

_____

_____

_____

Thursday, March 18, 2021

Fourth Week of Lent

JOHN 5:31-47

Jesus said to the Jews: "If I testify on my own behalf, my testimony is not true. But there is another who testifies on my behalf, and I know that the testimony he gives on my behalf is true. You sent emissaries to John, and he testified to the truth. I do not accept human testimony, but I say this so that you may be saved. He was a burning and shining lamp, and for a while you were content to rejoice in his light. But I have testimony greater than John's. The works that the Father gave me to accomplish, these works that I perform testify on my behalf that the Father has sent me. Moreover, the Father who sent me has testified on my behalf. But you have never heard his voice nor seen his form, and you do not have his word remaining in you, because you do not believe in the one whom he has sent. You search the Scriptures, because you think you have eternal life through them; even they testify on my behalf. But you do not want to come to me to have life.

"I do not accept human praise; moreover, I know that you do not have the love of God in you. I came in the name of my Father, but you do not accept me; yet if another comes in his own name, you will accept him. How can you believe, when you accept praise from one another and do not seek the praise that comes from the only God? Do not think that I will accuse you before the Father: the one who will accuse you is Moses in whom you have placed your hope. For if you had believed Moses, you would have believed me, because he wrote about me. But if you do not believe his writings, how will you believe my words?"

Friends, in today's Gospel, Jesus says that his Father's works testify to his identity. Jesus' words are the Father's words and his deeds are the Father's deeds. His story is the Father's story.

Nature speaks of God, the philosophers say true things about God, the arts can reflect him, the lives of the saints can indicate him—but Jesus is *the* Icon.

We sense in this passage, if I can put it this way, the humility of the Logos. Neither the words nor the deeds of Jesus are "his own." They are received from the Father. The Trinitarian theological tradition respects this when it speaks of the Son as the interior word of the Father and as having received everything from the Father.

REFLECT: How closely do your words and deeds align with Jesus' words and deeds? Would your words and deeds "convict" you of being a Christian?

Friday, March 19, 2021

Solemnity of Saint Joseph,
Husband of the Blessed Virgin Mary

MATTHEW 1:16, 18-21, 24A OR LUKE 2:41-51A

Jacob was the father of Joseph, the husband of Mary. Of her was born Jesus who is called the Christ.

Now this is how the birth of Jesus Christ came about. When his mother Mary was betrothed to Joseph, but before they lived together, she was found with child through the Holy Spirit. Joseph her husband, since he was a righteous man, yet unwilling to expose her to shame, decided to divorce her quietly. Such was his intention when, behold, the angel of the Lord appeared to him in a dream and said, "Joseph, son of David, do not be afraid to take Mary your wife into your home. For it is through the Holy Spirit that this child has been conceived in her. She will bear a son and you are to name him Jesus, because he will save his people from their sins." When Joseph awoke, he did as the angel of the Lord had commanded him and took his wife into his home.

Friends, today's Gospel centers on the intriguing figure of Joseph. Joseph is one of the most beloved of the saints, featured in countless works of art and prominent in the devotional lives of many.

We know almost nothing about him, yet some very powerful spiritual themes emerge in the accounts of Joseph. He had become betrothed to Mary, and this union had been blessed by God. And then he finds that his betrothed is pregnant.

This must have been an emotional maelstrom for him. And, at a deeper level, it is a spiritual crisis. What does God want him to do? Then the angel appears to him in a dream and tells him, "Joseph, son of David, do not be afraid to take Mary your wife into your home." He realizes at that moment that these puzzling events are part of a much greater plan of God's. What appears to be a disaster from his perspective is meaningful from God's perspective.

Joseph was willing to cooperate with the divine plan, though he in no way knew its contours or deepest purpose. Like Mary at the Annunciation, he trusted and let himself be led.

REFLECT: Think of a situation in your life that is out of your control. How much do you trust God and let yourself be led by him through this situation? Where do you have difficulties acting as Joseph did in this Gospel passage?

Saturday, March 20, 2021

Fourth Week of Lent

JOHN 7:40-53

Some in the crowd who heard these words of Jesus said, "This is truly the Prophet." Others said, "This is the Christ." But others said, "The Christ will not come from Galilee, will he? Does not Scripture say that the Christ will be of David's family and come from Bethlehem, the village where David lived?" So a division occurred in the crowd because of him. Some of them even wanted to arrest him, but no one laid hands on him.

So the guards went to the chief priests and Pharisees, who asked them, "Why did you not bring him?" The guards answered, "Never before has anyone spoken like this man." So the Pharisees answered them, "Have you also been deceived? Have any of the authorities or the Pharisees believed in him? But this crowd, which does not know the law, is accursed." Nicodemus, one of their members who had come to him earlier, said to them, "Does our law condemn a man before it first hears him and finds out what he is doing?" They answered and said

> to him, "You are not from Galilee also, are you?
> Look and see that no prophet arises from Galilee."
>
> Then each went to his own house.

Friends, we see in today's Gospel how Jesus' preaching caused division. Some hearers believed him, but others wanted to arrest him.

The life, preaching, and mission of Jesus are predicated upon the assumption that all is not well with us, that we stand in need of a renovation of vision, attitude, and behavior. A few decades ago the book *I'm OK—You're OK* appeared. Its title, and the attitude that it embodies, are inimical to Christianity.

The fact of sin is so often overlooked today. Look, no one has ever savored being accused of sin, but especially in our culture now there is an allergy to admitting personal fault.

A salvation religion makes no sense if all is basically fine with us, if all we need is a little sprucing up around the edges. Christian saints are those who can bear the awful revelation that sin is not simply an abstraction or something that other people wrestle with, but a power that lurks and works in them.

When we lose sight of sin, we lose sight of Christianity, which is a salvation religion.

REFLECT: Do you honestly believe that sin is a "power that lurks and works" in you? How often do you engage in a deep examination of conscience? How often do you receive the sacrament of Reconciliation?

_____

_____

_____

_____

_____

_____

_____

_____

_____

_____

_____

_____

_____

Sunday, March 21, 2021

Fifth Sunday of Lent

JOHN 12:20-33

Some Greeks who had come to worship at the Passover Feast came to Philip, who was from Bethsaida in Galilee, and asked him, "Sir, we would like to see Jesus." Philip went and told Andrew; then Andrew and Philip went and told Jesus. Jesus answered them, "The hour has come for the Son of Man to be glorified. Amen, amen, I say to you, unless a grain of wheat falls to the ground and dies, it remains just a grain of wheat; but if it dies, it produces much fruit. Whoever loves his life loses it, and whoever hates his life in this world will preserve it for eternal life. Whoever serves me must follow me, and where I am, there also will my servant be. The Father will honor whoever serves me.

"I am troubled now. Yet what should I say? 'Father, save me from this hour'? But it was for this purpose that I came to this hour. Father, glorify your name." Then a voice came from heaven, "I have glorified it and will glorify it again." The crowd there heard it and said it was thunder; but others said, "An angel has spoken to him." Jesus answered and said, "This voice did not come for my sake but for yours. Now is the time of judgment on this world; now the ruler of this world will be driven out. And when I am lifted up from the earth, I will draw everyone to myself." He said this indicating the kind of death he would die.

Friends, our Gospel for today contains one of the most beautiful and terrible summations of the Christian message: "Amen, amen, I say to you, unless a grain of wheat falls to the ground and dies, it remains just a grain of wheat; but if it dies, it produces much fruit."

And now this one upon whom the crowds had pinned their hopes is speaking of falling to the earth and dying. And then it gets stranger. "Whoever loves his life loses it, and whoever hates his life in this world will preserve it for eternal life." Come again?!

Just when we are raising you up, you're talking about falling down; just when we are showing you that your life has come to its fulfillment, you're talking about hating this life.

To understand what all this means, we should go back to the grain of wheat that falls to the earth. A seed's life is inside, yes, but it's a life that grows by being given away and mixing with the soil around it. It has to crack open, to be destroyed.

Jesus' sign is the sign of the cross—the death that leads to transfiguration.

Reflect: What are the characteristics of someone who loves her life in this world? What are the characteristics of someone who hates his life in this world? Which are you?

_____

_____

_____

_____

_____

_____

_____

_____

_____

_____

_____

_____

Monday, March 22, 2021

Fifth Week of Lent

JOHN 8:1-11

Jesus went to the Mount of Olives. But early in the morning he arrived again in the temple area, and all the people started coming to him, and he sat down and taught them. Then the scribes and the Pharisees brought a woman who had been caught in adultery and made her stand in the middle. They said to him, "Teacher, this woman was caught in the very act of committing adultery. Now in the law, Moses commanded us to stone such women. So what do you say?" They said this to test him, so that they could have some charge to bring against him. Jesus bent down and began to write on the ground with his finger. But when they continued asking him, he straightened up and said to them, "Let the one among you who is without sin be the first to throw a stone at her." Again he bent down and wrote on the ground. And in response, they went away one by one, beginning with the elders. So he was left alone with the woman before him. Then Jesus straightened up and said to her, "Woman, where are they? Has no one condemned you?" She replied, "No one, sir." Then Jesus said, "Neither do I condemn you. Go, and from now on do not sin any more."

Friends, today's Gospel presents the story of the woman caught in adultery, which is one of the clearest demonstrations of what René Girard called the scapegoat mechanism.

The scribes and Pharisees bring to Jesus a woman who had been caught in adultery. The novelty of the Gospel is revealed in Jesus' refusal to contribute to the energy of the gathering storm: "Let the one among you who is without sin be the first to throw a stone at her." Jesus directs the energy of scapegoating violence back toward the accusers. He unveils the dangerous secret that the unstable order of the society has been predicated upon scapegoating. The Church Fathers emphasized this point with a neat interpretive move: they imagined that Jesus was writing in the sand none other than the sins of those who were threatening the woman.

Then we see, at least in seminal form, the new order: "Go, and from now on do not sin any more." The connection between Jesus and the woman is not the consequence of condemnation but rather the fruit of forgiveness offered and accepted.

REFLECT: Reflect on the prevalence of scapegoating in contemporary culture. Think especially about the times when you have been guilty of singling out an individual or some group as a scapegoat.

Tuesday, March 23, 2021

Fifth Week of Lent

Jesus said to the Pharisees: "I am going away and you will look for me, but you will die in your sin. Where I am going you cannot come." So the Jews said, "He is not going to kill himself, is he, because he said, 'Where I am going you cannot come'?" He said to them, "You belong to what is below, I belong to what is above. You belong to this world, but I do not belong to this world. That is why I told you that you will die in your sins. For if you do not believe that I AM, you will die in your sins." So they said to him, "Who are you?" Jesus said to them, "What I told you from the beginning. I have much to say about you in condemnation. But the one who sent me is true, and what I heard from him I tell the world." They did not realize that he was speaking to them of the Father. So Jesus said to them, "When you lift up the Son of Man, then you will realize that I AM, and that I do nothing on my own, but I say only what the Father taught me. The one who sent me is with me. He has not left me alone, because I always do what is pleasing to him." Because he spoke this way, many came to believe in him.

Friends, in today's Gospel, Jesus prophesies his Crucifixion and his Father's role in his coming death. What enabled the first Christians to hold up the cross, to sing its praises, to wear it as a decoration is the fact that God raised up and ratified precisely this crucified Jesus. "You killed him, but God raised him up." Therefore, God was involved in this terrible thing; God was there, working out his salvific purposes.

But what does this mean? There have been numerous attempts throughout the Christian centuries to name the salvific nature of the cross. Let me offer just one take on it. It became clear to the first Christians that somehow, on that terrible cross, sin had been dealt with. The curse of sin had been removed, taken care of. On that terrible cross, Jesus functioned as the "Lamb of God," sacrificed for sin.

Does this mean God the Father is a cruel taskmaster demanding a bloody sacrifice so that his anger might be appeased? No, Jesus' Crucifixion was the opening up of the divine heart so that we could see that no sin of ours could finally separate us from the love of God.

REFLECT: Do you acknowledge and accept that the penalty of sin is death? Given your perspective, then, how do you understand the death of Jesus on the cross?

Wednesday, March 24, 2021

Fifth Week of Lent

JOHN 8:31-42

Jesus said to those Jews who believed in him, "If you remain in my word, you will truly be my disciples, and you will know the truth, and the truth will set you free." They answered him, "We are descendants of Abraham and have never been enslaved to anyone. How can you say, 'You will become free'?" Jesus answered them, "Amen, amen, I say to you, everyone who commits sin is a slave of sin. A slave does not remain in a household forever, but a son always remains. So if the Son frees you, then you will truly be free. I know that you are descendants of Abraham. But you are trying to kill me, because my word has no room among you. I tell you what I have seen in the Father's presence; then do what you have heard from the Father."

They answered and said to him, "Our father is Abraham." Jesus said to them, "If you were Abraham's children, you would be doing the works of Abraham. But now you are trying to kill me, a man who has told you the truth that I heard from God; Abraham did not do this. You are doing the works of your father!" So they said to him, "We were not born of fornication. We have one Father, God." Jesus said to them, "If God were your Father, you would love me, for I came from God and am here; I did not come on my own, but he sent me."

Friends, today in our Gospel, Jesus confronts those Jewish leaders who want to kill him, telling them that they are hardened in their sin. He speaks: "Amen, amen, I say to you, everyone who commits sin is a slave of sin."

In our tradition, sin is a kind of nonbeing, an illusion, if you will. To live in sin is to live stubbornly in an unreal world. Our mind becomes confused, and our will disoriented. This helps explain why the devil is often referred to as the father of lies.

Theologian Henri de Lubac gives voice to this conviction when he refers to sin as *cette claudication mystérieuse*, this mysterious limp. It is a deformation, a corruption.

All of us sinners have, to one degree or another, bought into the lie. At the heart of the lie—and we can see it in the Genesis account—is the deification of the ego. I become the center of the universe, I with my needs and my fears and my demands.

And when the puny "I" is the center of the cosmos, the tie that binds all things to one another is lost. The basic reality now becomes rivalry, competition, violence, and mistrust.

REFLECT: What is the "tie that binds all things to one another"? How does sin or the "deification of the ego" damage this bond?

_____

_____

_____

_____

_____

_____

_____

_____

_____

_____

_____

_____

_____

_____

_____

_____

Thursday, March 25, 2021

Solemnity of the Annunciation of the Lord

The angel Gabriel was sent from God to a town of Galilee called Nazareth, to a virgin betrothed to a man named Joseph, of the house of David, and the virgin's name was Mary. And coming to her, he said, "Hail, full of grace! The Lord is with you." But she was greatly troubled at what was said and pondered what sort of greeting this might be. Then the angel said to her, "Do not be afraid, Mary, for you have found favor with God. Behold, you will conceive in your womb and bear a son, and you shall name him Jesus. He will be great and will be called Son of the Most High, and the Lord God will give him the throne of David his father, and he will rule over the house of Jacob forever, and of his Kingdom there will be no end." But Mary said to the angel, "How can this be, since I have no relations with a man?"And the angel said to her in reply, "The Holy Spirit will come upon you, and the power of the Most High will overshadow you. Therefore the child to be born will be called holy, the Son of God. And behold, Elizabeth, your relative, has also conceived a son in her old age, and this is the sixth month for her who was called barren; for nothing will be impossible for God." Mary said, "Behold, I am the handmaid of the Lord. May it be done to me according to your word." Then the angel departed from her.

Friends, in today's Gospel, the angel Gabriel reveals to Mary that she will bear a Son who will reign from David's throne.

As background, note that God had promised that David's throne would last forever, but his line had apparently been broken in 587 BC. Six hundred years later Gabriel appeared to Mary, who was betrothed to a man named Joseph of the house of David.

Greeting her as "full of grace," the angel announced that she will conceive in her womb and bear a Son. "He will be great and will be called Son of the Most High." Then comes the kicker that would have taken the breath away from any first-century Jew listening to the story: "And the Lord God will give him the throne of David his father, and he will rule over the house of Jacob forever, and of his Kingdom there will be no end."

What seemed to have come to an end had in fact just gone underground, and was now ready to appear fully in the light. The kingly line of David was in fact unsevered, and now the full meaning of God's promise would be revealed.

REFLECT: How does the truth that Gabriel spoke—"nothing will be impossible for God"—affect you and your prayer life?

_____

_____

_____

_____

_____

_____

_____

_____

_____

_____

_____

_____

_____

_____

_____

Friday, March 26, 2021

Fifth Week of Lent

JOHN 10:31-42

The Jews picked up rocks to stone Jesus. Jesus answered them, "I have shown you many good works from my Father. For which of these are you trying to stone me?" The Jews answered him, "We are not stoning you for a good work but for blasphemy. You, a man, are making yourself God." Jesus answered them, "Is it not written in your law, 'I said, 'You are gods'"? If it calls them gods to whom the word of God came, and Scripture cannot be set aside, can you say that the one whom the Father has consecrated and sent into the world blasphemes because I said, 'I am the Son of God'? If I do not perform my Father's works, do not believe me; but if I perform them, even if you do not believe me, believe the works, so that you may realize and understand that the Father is in me and I am in the Father." Then they tried again to arrest him; but he escaped from their power.

He went back across the Jordan to the place where John first baptized, and there he remained. Many came to him and said, "John performed no sign, but everything John said about this man was true." And many there began to believe in him.

Friends, in today's Gospel, Jewish leaders attempt to stone Jesus because he claimed to be the Son of God. He defended his identity, saying, "If I do not perform my Father's works, do not believe me; but if I perform them, even if you do not believe me, believe the works, so that you may realize and understand that the Father is in me and I am in the Father."

At the Last Supper, Jesus would further explain his intimate relationship with the Father. There he lays out for us the coinherence that obtains at the most fundamental dimension of being—that is to say, within the very existence of God. "Master," Philip said to him, "Show us the Father, and that will be enough for us." Jesus replied, "Have I been with you for so long a time and you still do not know me, Philip? Whoever has seen me has seen the Father."

How can this be true, unless the Father and the Son coinhere in each other? Though Father and Son are truly distinct, they are utterly implicated in each other by a mutual act of love. As Jesus says, "The Father who dwells in me is doing his works."

REFLECT: Jesus argues that his identity should be clear from his works. What would those around you say is your identity, if they only knew of you through your works? How prominent would Christianity be in your perceived identity?

Saturday, March 27, 2021

Fifth Week of Lent

JOHN 11:45-56

Many of the Jews who had come to Mary and seen what Jesus had done began to believe in him. But some of them went to the Pharisees and told them what Jesus had done. So the chief priests and the Pharisees convened the Sanhedrin and said, "What are we going to do? This man is performing many signs. If we leave him alone, all will believe in him, and the Romans will come and take away both our land and our nation." But one of them, Caiaphas, who was high priest that year, said to them, "You know nothing, nor do you consider that it is better for you that one man should die instead of the people, so that the whole nation may not perish." He did not say this on his own, but since he was high priest for that year, he prophesied that Jesus was going to die for the nation, and not only for the nation, but also to gather into one the dispersed children of God. So from that day on they planned to kill him.

So Jesus no longer walked about in public among the Jews, but he left for the region near the desert, to a town called Ephraim, and there he remained with his disciples.

> Now the Passover of the Jews was near, and many went up from the country to Jerusalem before Passover to purify themselves. They looked for Jesus and said to one another as they were in the temple area, "What do you think? That he will not come to the feast?"

Friends, in today's Gospel, the Pharisees plot to kill Jesus because he raised Lazarus. Once again, we see here a particular form of opposition—namely, scapegoating. René Girard identified the scapegoating mechanism as basic to the maintenance of order in most human communities. When tensions arise among people due to competitive desire, scapegoats—usually outsiders—are automatically singled out, and upon them is cast the collective anxiety of the group.

The leaders of the nation are seeking to isolate and eliminate Jesus because they are anxious to soothe tensions among the people. The author of John's Gospel stresses this dimension when he puts in the mouth of Caiaphas these words: "You know nothing, nor do you consider that it is better for you that one man should die instead of the people, so that the whole nation may not perish."

But, in Jesus, the true God will undermine this officially sanctioned scapegoating by becoming the scapegoat himself.

REFLECT: How did the Resurrection turn the scapegoating that Caiaphas supported into the key to our salvation?

_____

_____

_____

_____

_____

_____

_____

_____

_____

_____

_____

_____

_____

_____

_____

_____

Sunday, March 28, 2021

Palm Sunday of the Lord's Passion

MARK 14:1-15:47 OR MARK 15:1-39

The Passover and the Feast of Unleavened Bread were to take place in two days' time. So the chief priests and the scribes were seeking a way to arrest him by treachery and put him to death. They said, "Not during the festival, for fear that there may be a riot among the people."

When he was in Bethany reclining at table in the house of Simon the leper, a woman came with an alabaster jar of perfumed oil, costly genuine spikenard. She broke the alabaster jar and poured it on his head. There were some who were indignant. "Why has there been this waste of perfumed oil? It could have been sold for more than three hundred days' wages and the money given to the poor." They were infuriated with her. Jesus said, "Let her alone. Why do you make trouble for her? She has done a good thing for me. The poor you will always have with you, and whenever you wish you can do good to them, but you will not always have me. She has done what she could. She has anticipated anointing my body for burial. Amen, I say to you, wherever the gospel is proclaimed to the whole world, what she has done will be told in memory of her."

Then Judas Iscariot, one of the Twelve, went off to the chief priests to hand him over to them. When they heard him they were pleased and promised to pay him money. Then he looked for an opportunity to hand him over.

On the first day of the Feast of Unleavened Bread, when they sacrificed the Passover lamb, his disciples said to him, "Where do you want us to go and prepare for you to eat the Passover?" He sent two of his disciples and said to them, "Go into the city and a man will meet you, carrying a jar of water. Follow him. Wherever he enters, say to the master of the house, 'The Teacher says, "Where is my guest room where I may eat the Passover with my disciples?"' Then he will show you a large upper room furnished and ready. Make the preparations for us there." The disciples then went off, entered the city, and found it just as he had told them; and they prepared the Passover.

When it was evening, he came with the Twelve. And as they reclined at table and were eating, Jesus said, "Amen, I say to you, one of you will betray me, one who is eating with me." They began to be distressed and to say to him, one by one, "Surely it is not I?" He said to them, "One of the Twelve, the one who dips with me into the dish. For the Son of Man indeed goes, as it is written of him, but woe to that man by whom the Son of Man is betrayed. It would be better for that man if he had never been born."

While they were eating, he took bread, said the blessing, broke it, and gave it to them, and said, "Take it; this is my body." Then he took a cup, gave thanks, and gave it to them, and they all drank from it. He said to them, "This is my blood of the covenant, which will be shed for many. Amen, I say to you, I shall not drink again the fruit of the vine until the day when I drink it new in the kingdom of God." Then, after singing a hymn, they went out to the Mount of Olives.

Then Jesus said to them, "All of you will have your faith shaken, for it is written:
I will strike the shepherd,
and the sheep will be dispersed.
But after I have been raised up, I shall go before you to Galilee." Peter said to him, "Even though all should have their faith shaken, mine will not be." Then Jesus said to him, "Amen, I say to you, this very night before the cock crows twice you will deny me three times." But he vehemently replied, "Even though I should have to die with you, I will not deny you." And they all spoke similarly.

Then they came to a place named Gethsemane, and he said to his disciples, "Sit here while I pray."

He took with him Peter, James, and John, and began to be troubled and distressed. Then he said to them, "My soul is sorrowful even to death. Remain here and keep watch." He advanced a little and fell to the ground and prayed that if it were possible the hour might pass by him; he said, "Abba, Father, all things are possible to you. Take this cup away from me, but not what I will but what you will." When he returned he found them asleep. He said to Peter, "Simon, are you asleep? Could you not keep watch for one hour? Watch and pray that you may not undergo the test. The spirit is willing but the flesh is weak." Withdrawing again, he prayed, saying the same thing. Then he returned once more and found them asleep, for they could not keep their eyes open and did not know what to answer him. He returned a third time and said to them, "Are you still sleeping and taking your rest? It is enough. The hour has come. Behold, the Son of Man is to be handed over to sinners. Get up, let us go. See, my betrayer is at hand."

Then, while he was still speaking, Judas, one of the Twelve, arrived, accompanied by a crowd with swords and clubs who had come from the chief priests, the scribes, and the elders. His betrayer had arranged a signal with them, saying, "The man I shall kiss is the one; arrest him and lead him away securely." He came and immediately went over to him and said, "Rabbi." And he kissed him. At this they laid hands on him and arrested him. One of the bystanders drew his sword, struck the high priest's servant, and cut off his ear. Jesus said to them in reply, "Have you come out as against a robber, with swords and clubs, to seize me? Day after day I was with you teaching in the temple area, yet you did not arrest me; but that the Scriptures may be fulfilled." And they all left him and fled. Now a young man followed him wearing nothing but a linen cloth about his body. They seized him, but he left the cloth behind and ran off naked.

They led Jesus away to the high priest, and all the chief priests and the elders and the scribes came together. Peter followed him at a distance into the high priest's courtyard and was seated with the guards, warming himself at the fire. The chief priests and the entire Sanhedrin kept trying to obtain testimony against Jesus in order to put him to death, but they found none. Many gave false witness against him, but their testimony did not agree. Some took the stand and testified falsely against him, alleging, "We heard him say, 'I will destroy this temple made with hands and within three days I will build another not made with hands.'" Even so their testimony did not agree. The high priest rose before the assembly

and questioned Jesus, saying, "Have you no answer? What are these men testifying against you?" But he was silent and answered nothing. Again the high priest asked him and said to him, "Are you the Christ, the son of the Blessed One?" Then Jesus answered, "I am;
and 'you will see the Son of Man
seated at the right hand of the Power
and coming with the clouds of heaven.'"
At that the high priest tore his garments and said, "What further need have we of witnesses? You have heard the blasphemy. What do you think?" They all condemned him as deserving to die. Some began to spit on him. They blindfolded him and struck him and said to him, "Prophesy!" And the guards greeted him with blows.

While Peter was below in the courtyard, one of the high priest's maids came along. Seeing Peter warming himself, she looked intently at him and said, "You too were with the Nazarene, Jesus." But he denied it saying, "I neither know nor understand what you are talking about." So he went out into the outer court. Then the cock crowed. The maid saw him and began again to say to the bystanders, "This man is one of them." Once again he denied it. A little later the bystanders said to Peter once more, "Surely you are one of them; for you too are a Galilean." He began to curse and to swear, "I do not know this man about whom you are talking." And immediately a cock crowed a second time. Then Peter remembered the word that Jesus had said to him, "Before the cock crows twice you will deny me three times."He broke down and wept.

As soon as morning came, the chief priests with the elders and the scribes, that is, the whole Sanhedrin held a council. They bound Jesus, led him away, and handed him over to Pilate. Pilate questioned him, "Are you the king of the Jews?" He said to him in reply, "You say so." The chief priests accused him of many things. Again Pilate questioned him, "Have you no answer? See how many things they accuse you of." Jesus gave him no further answer, so that Pilate was amazed.

Now on the occasion of the feast he used to release to them one prisoner whom they requested. A man called Barabbas was then in prison along with the rebels who had committed murder in a rebellion. The crowd came forward and began to ask him to do for them as he was accustomed. Pilate answered, "Do you want me to release to you the king of the Jews?" For he knew that it was out of envy that the chief priests had handed him over. But the chief priests stirred up the crowd to have him release Barabbas for them instead. Pilate again said to them in reply, "Then what do you want me to do with the man you call the king of the Jews?" They shouted again, "Crucify him." Pilate said to them, "Why? What evil has he done?" They only shouted the louder, "Crucify him." So Pilate, wishing to satisfy the crowd, released Barabbas to them and, after he had Jesus scourged, handed him over to be crucified.

The soldiers led him away inside the palace, that is, the praetorium, and assembled the whole cohort. They clothed him in purple and, weaving a crown of thorns, placed it on him. They began to salute him with, "Hail, King of the Jews!" and kept striking his head with a reed and spitting upon him. They knelt before him in homage. And when they had mocked him, they stripped him of the purple cloak, dressed him in his own clothes, and led him out to crucify him.

They pressed into service a passer-by, Simon, a Cyrenian, who was coming in from the country, the father of Alexander and Rufus, to carry his cross.

They brought him to the place of Golgotha—which is translated Place of the Skull—. They gave him wine drugged with myrrh, but he did not take it. Then they crucified him and divided his garments by casting lots for them to see what each should take. It was nine o'clock in the morning when they crucified him. The inscription of the charge against him read, "The King of the Jews." With him they crucified two revolutionaries, one on his right and one on his left. Those passing by reviled him, shaking their heads and saying, "Aha! You who would destroy the temple and rebuild it in three days, save yourself by coming down from the cross." Likewise the chief priests, with the scribes, mocked him among themselves and said, "He saved others; he cannot save himself. Let the Christ, the King of Israel, come down now from the cross that we may see and believe." Those who were crucified with him also kept abusing him.

At noon darkness came over the whole land until three in the afternoon. And at three o'clock Jesus cried out in a loud voice, *"Eloi, Eloi, lema sabachthani?"* which is translated, "My God, my God, why have you forsaken me?" Some of the bystanders who heard it said, "Look, he is calling Elijah." One of them ran, soaked a sponge with wine, put it on a reed and gave it to him to drink saying, "Wait, let us see if Elijah comes to take him down." Jesus gave a loud cry and breathed his last.

Here all kneel and pause for a short time.

The veil of the sanctuary was torn in two from top to bottom. When the centurion who stood facing him saw how he breathed his last he said, "Truly this man was the Son of God!" There were also women looking on from a distance. Among them were Mary Magdalene, Mary the mother of the younger James and of Joses, and Salome. These women had followed him when he was in Galilee and ministered to him. There were also many other women who had come up with him to Jerusalem.

When it was already evening, since it was the day of preparation, the day before the sabbath, Joseph of Arimathea, a distinguished member of the council, who was himself awaiting the kingdom of God, came and courageously went to Pilate and asked for the body of Jesus. Pilate was amazed that he was already dead. He summoned the centurion and asked him if Jesus had already died. And when he learned of it from the centurion, he gave the body to Joseph. Having bought a linen cloth, he took him down, wrapped him in the linen cloth, and laid him in a tomb that had been hewn out of the rock. Then he rolled a stone against the entrance to the tomb. Mary Magdalene and Mary the mother of Joses watched where he was laid.

Friends, on this Palm Sunday, we are privileged to become immersed in Mark's great Passion narrative, where the kingship of Jesus emerges with great clarity—and also with great irony.

We read that upon being brought before the Sanhedrin, Jesus is asked whether he is the "Christ,"—that is, the Messiah—an implicit reference to David. When Jesus calmly responds, "I am," the high priest tears his robes, for how could a shackled criminal possibly be the kingly descendant of David? Upon being presented to Pilate, Jesus is asked the functionally equivalent question: "Are you the king of the Jews?" Again a blandly affirmative answer comes: "You say so." This leads the soldiers to mock him, placing a purple cloak on his shoulders and a crown of thorns on his head.

Mark does not want us to miss the irony that, precisely as the King of the Jews and the Son of David, Jesus is implicitly King to those soldiers. For the mission of the Davidic king is the unification not only of the tribes of Israel but also of the tribes of the world. What commenced with David's gathering of the tribes of Israel would soon reach completion in the criminal raised high on the cross, thereby drawing all people to himself.

REFLECT: Meditate on one of Christianity's most mysterious truths: that the Crucifixion of the Son of God was the means of our redemption.

Monday, March 29, 2021

Monday of Holy Week

JOHN 12:1-11

Six days before Passover Jesus came to Bethany, where Lazarus was, whom Jesus had raised from the dead. They gave a dinner for him there, and Martha served, while Lazarus was one of those reclining at table with him. Mary took a liter of costly perfumed oil made from genuine aromatic nard and anointed the feet of Jesus and dried them with her hair; the house was filled with the fragrance of the oil. Then Judas the Iscariot, one of his disciples, and the one who would betray him, said, "Why was this oil not sold for three hundred days' wages and given to the poor?" He said this not because he cared about the poor but because he was a thief and held the money bag and used to steal the contributions. So Jesus said, "Leave her alone. Let her keep this for the day of my burial. You always have the poor with you, but you do not always have me."

The large crowd of the Jews found out that he was there and came, not only because of him, but also to see Lazarus, whom he had raised from the dead. And the chief priests plotted to kill Lazarus too, because many of the Jews were turning away and believing in Jesus because of him.

LENTEN *GOSPEL* REFLECTIONS

Friends, in today's Gospel, Mary of Bethany anoints Jesus for his death and burial. By this act, she anticipates the visit of three women to the tomb of Jesus. Early on the morning of the first day of the week, Mary Magdalene, Mary the Mother of James, and Salome will bring spices to anoint the body of Jesus.

They will look in and see a young man—and be frightened out of their wits. Can you imagine? You walk into a tomb, fully expecting to see a dead body, and you see instead someone alive and well—someone different than the man who was buried there! But that will not be the end of their surprise. The man will announce that the Jesus whom they seek is not there, that he has been raised up and will go ahead of them into Galilee.

From this grave of Jesus we will learn that everything we took to be the case is not the case. God is the enemy of death, and he has shown us his power over death in the most unambiguous way; our lives no longer need to be dominated by the fear of death, and we see the proof of this in the most vivid way imaginable.

Keep all of that in mind as we read this beautiful story of Mary of Bethany anointing the feet of Jesus.

REFLECT: How do you feel about your own death? Why?

Tuesday, March 30, 2021

Tuesday of Holy Week

JOHN 13:21-33,36-38

Reclining at table with his disciples, Jesus was deeply troubled and testified, "Amen, amen, I say to you, one of you will betray me." The disciples looked at one another, at a loss as to whom he meant. One of his disciples, the one whom Jesus loved, was reclining at Jesus' side. So Simon Peter nodded to him to find out whom he meant. He leaned back against Jesus' chest and said to him, "Master, who is it?" Jesus answered, "It is the one to whom I hand the morsel after I have dipped it." So he dipped the morsel and took it and handed it to Judas, son of Simon the Iscariot. After Judas took the morsel, Satan entered him. So Jesus said to him, "What you are going to do, do quickly." Now none of those reclining at table realized why he said this to him. Some thought that since Judas kept the money bag, Jesus had told him, "Buy what we need for the feast," or to give something to the poor. So Judas took the morsel and left at once. And it was night.

When he had left, Jesus said, "Now is the Son of Man glorified, and God is glorified in him. If God is glorified in him, God will also glorify him in himself, and he will glorify him at once. My children, I will be with you only a little while longer. You will look for me, and as I told the Jews, 'Where I go you cannot come,' so now I say it to you."

Simon Peter said to him, "Master, where are you going?" Jesus answered him, "Where I am going, you cannot follow me now, though you will follow later." Peter said to him, "Master, why can I not follow you now? I will lay down my life for you." Jesus answered, "Will you lay down your life for me? Amen, amen, I say to you, the cock will not crow before you deny me three times."

Friends, today's Gospel is from John's account of the Last Supper, where Jesus acknowledges Judas as his betrayer and tells him to get on with it.

God's desires have been, from the beginning, opposed. Consistently, human beings have preferred the isolation of sin to the festivity of the sacred meal. Theologians have called this anomalous tendency the *mysterium iniquitatis* (the mystery of evil), for there is no rational ground for it, no reason for it to exist.

But there it stubbornly is, always shadowing the good, parasitic upon that which it tries to destroy. Therefore, we should not be too surprised that, as the sacred meal comes to its richest possible expression, evil accompanies it.

Judas the betrayer expresses the *mysterium iniquitatis* with particular symbolic power, for he had spent years in intimacy with Jesus, taking in the Lord's moves and thoughts at close quarters, sharing the table of fellowship with him—and yet he saw fit to turn Jesus over to his enemies and to interrupt the coinherence of the Last Supper.

Those of us who regularly gather around the table of intimacy with Christ and yet engage consistently in the works of darkness are meant to see ourselves in the betrayer.

REFLECT: When have you been confronted with the "mystery of evil," and what role did your faith play in processing that confrontation?

_____

_____

_____

_____

_____

_____

_____

Wednesday, March 31, 2021

Wednesday of Holy Week

MATTHEW 26:14-25

One of the Twelve, who was called Judas Iscariot, went to the chief priests and said, "What are you willing to give me if I hand him over to you?" They paid him thirty pieces of silver, and from that time on he looked for an opportunity to hand him over.

On the first day of the Feast of Unleavened Bread, the disciples approached Jesus and said, "Where do you want us to prepare for you to eat the Passover?" He said, "Go into the city to a certain man and tell him, 'The teacher says, My appointed time draws near; in your house I shall celebrate the Passover with my disciples.'" The disciples then did as Jesus had ordered, and prepared the Passover.

When it was evening, he reclined at table with the Twelve. And while they were eating, he said, "Amen, I say to you, one of you will betray me." Deeply distressed at this, they began to say to him one after another, "Surely it is not I, Lord?" He said in reply, "He who has dipped his hand into the dish with me is the one who will betray me. The Son of Man indeed goes, as it is written of him, but woe to that man by whom the Son of Man is betrayed. It would be better for that man if he had never been born."

> Then Judas, his betrayer, said in reply, "Surely it is not I, Rabbi?" He answered, "You have said so."

Friends, in today's Gospel, Jesus asks his disciples to go into Jerusalem and prepare a Passover supper.

At the heart of the Passover meal was the eating of a lamb, which had been sacrificed, in remembrance of the lambs of the original Passover whose blood had been smeared on the doorposts of the Israelites in Egypt. Making his Last Supper a Passover meal, Jesus was signaling the fulfillment of John the Baptist's prophecy that he, Jesus, would be the Lamb of God and the definitive sacrifice.

This sacrifice is made sacramentally present at every Mass—not for the sake of God, who has no need of it, but for our sake. In the Mass, we participate in the act by which divinity and humanity are reconciled, and we eat the sacrificed Body and drink the poured-out Blood of the Lamb of God.

REFLECT: In prayer, enter deeply into the sacrifice of Jesus as the Lamb of God. What was his suffering like? What did it accomplish?

Thursday, April 1, 2021

Holy Thursday — Chrism Mass

LUKE 4:16-21

Jesus came to Nazareth, where he had grown up, and went according to his custom into the synagogue on the sabbath day. He stood up to read and was handed a scroll of the prophet Isaiah. He unrolled the scroll and found the passage where it was written:

The Spirit of the Lord is upon me,
because he has anointed me
to bring glad tidings to the poor.
He has sent me to proclaim liberty to captives
and recovery of sight to the blind,
to let the oppressed go free,
and to proclaim a year acceptable to the Lord.

Rolling up the scroll, he handed it back to the attendant and sat down, and the eyes of all in the synagogue looked intently at him. He said to them, "Today this Scripture passage is fulfilled in your hearing."

LENTEN *GOSPEL* REFLECTIONS

Friends, today's Gospel recounts Jesus' inaugural address in his hometown synagogue. Jesus reads words from the prophet Isaiah that he felt best summed up who he was and what his mission was. Therefore, it behooves us to listen carefully.

Jesus first says, "The Spirit of the Lord is upon me." The *Ruach Yahweh*, the breath of God, the Spirit that hovered over the surface of the waters at the beginning of time, the life energy of God—this is what has seized and animated Jesus.

Animated by the *Ruach Yahweh*, what does Jesus do? He brings "glad tidings to the poor," "liberty to captives," and "recovery of sight to the blind." In other words, he brings God's love to those who are marginalized by injustice, freedom to those who are imprisoned in sin, and healing to those whose very self has been broken.

After the Paschal Mystery and Resurrection, he breathed on his disciples, communicating to them something of this Spirit—and drawing them into this mission.

REFLECT: How has Jesus brought God's love to you?

_____

_____

_____

_____

_____

Friday, April 2, 2021

Good Friday of the Lord's Passion

JOHN 18:1-19:42

Jesus went out with his disciples across the Kidron valley to where there was a garden, into which he and his disciples entered. Judas his betrayer also knew the place, because Jesus had often met there with his disciples. So Judas got a band of soldiers and guards from the chief priests and the Pharisees and went there with lanterns, torches, and weapons. Jesus, knowing everything that was going to happen to him, went out and said to them, "Whom are you looking for?" They answered him, "Jesus the Nazorean." He said to them, "I AM." Judas his betrayer was also with them. When he said to them, "I AM, " they turned away and fell to the ground. So he again asked them, "Whom are you looking for?" They said, "Jesus the Nazorean." Jesus answered, "I told you that I AM. So if you are looking for me, let these men go." This was to fulfill what he had said, "I have not lost any of those you gave me." Then Simon Peter, who had a sword, drew it, struck the high priest's slave, and cut off his right ear. The slave's name was Malchus. Jesus said to Peter, "Put your sword into its scabbard. Shall I not drink the cup that the Father gave me?"

So the band of soldiers, the tribune, and the Jewish guards seized Jesus, bound him, and brought him to Annas first. He was the father-in-law of Caiaphas, who was high priest that year. It was Caiaphas who had counseled the Jews that it was better that one man should die rather than the people.

Simon Peter and another disciple followed Jesus. Now the other disciple was known to the high priest, and he entered the courtyard of the high priest with Jesus. But Peter stood at the gate outside. So the other disciple, the acquaintance of the high priest, went out and spoke to the gatekeeper and brought Peter in. Then the maid who was the gatekeeper said to Peter, "You are not one of this man's disciples, are you?" He said, "I am not." Now the slaves and the guards were standing around a charcoal fire that they had made, because it was cold, and were warming themselves. Peter was also standing there keeping warm.

The high priest questioned Jesus about his disciples and about his doctrine. Jesus answered him, "I have spoken publicly to the world. I have always taught in a synagogue or in the temple area where all the Jews gather, and in secret I have said nothing.

Why ask me? Ask those who heard me what I said to them. They know what I said." When he had said this, one of the temple guards standing there struck Jesus and said, "Is this the way you answer the high priest?" Jesus answered him, "If I have spoken wrongly, testify to the wrong; but if I have spoken rightly, why do you strike me?" Then Annas sent him bound to Caiaphas the high priest.

Now Simon Peter was standing there keeping warm. And they said to him, "You are not one of his disciples, are you?" He denied it and said, "I am not." One of the slaves of the high priest, a relative of the one whose ear Peter had cut off, said, "Didn't I see you in the garden with him?" Again Peter denied it. And immediately the cock crowed.

Then they brought Jesus from Caiaphas to the praetorium. It was morning. And they themselves did not enter the praetorium, in order not to be defiled so that they could eat the Passover. So Pilate came out to them and said, "What charge do you bring against this man?" They answered and said to him, "If he were not a criminal, we would not have handed him over to you." At this, Pilate said to them, "Take him yourselves, and judge him according to your law." The Jews answered him, "We do not have the right to execute anyone, " in order that the word of Jesus might be fulfilled that he said indicating the kind of death he would die. So Pilate went back into the praetorium and summoned Jesus and said to him, "Are you the King of the Jews?" Jesus answered, "Do you say this on your own or have others told you about me?" Pilate answered, "I am not a Jew, am I? Your own nation and the chief priests handed you over to me. What have you done?" Jesus answered, "My kingdom does not belong to this world. If my kingdom did belong to this world, my attendants would be fighting to keep me from being handed over to the Jews. But as it is, my kingdom is not here." So Pilate said to him, "Then you are a king?" Jesus answered, "You say I am a king. For this I was born and for this I came into the world, to testify to the truth. Everyone who belongs to the truth listens to my voice." Pilate said to him, "What is truth?"

When he had said this, he again went out to the Jews and said to them, "I find no guilt in him. But you have a custom that I release one prisoner to you at Passover. Do you want me to release to you the King of the Jews?" They cried out again, "Not this one but

Barabbas!" Now Barabbas was a revolutionary.

Then Pilate took Jesus and had him scourged. And the soldiers wove a crown out of thorns and placed it on his head, and clothed him in a purple cloak, and they came to him and said, "Hail, King of the Jews!" And they struck him repeatedly. Once more Pilate went out and said to them, "Look, I am bringing him out to you, so that you may know that I find no guilt in him." So Jesus came out, wearing the crown of thorns and the purple cloak. And he said to them, "Behold, the man!" When the chief priests and the guards saw him they cried out, "Crucify him, crucify him!" Pilate said to them, "Take him yourselves and crucify him. I find no guilt in him." The Jews answered, "We have a law, and according to that law he ought to die, because he made himself the Son of God." Now when Pilate heard this statement, he became even more afraid, and went back into the praetorium and said to Jesus, "Where are you from?" Jesus did not answer him. So Pilate said to him, "Do you not speak to me? Do you not know that I have power to release you and I have power to crucify you?" Jesus answered him, "You would have no power over me if it had not been given to you from above. For this reason the one who handed me over to you has the greater sin." Consequently, Pilate tried to release him; but the Jews cried out, "If you release him, you are not a Friend of Caesar. Everyone who makes himself a king opposes Caesar."

When Pilate heard these words he brought Jesus out and seated him on the judge's bench in the place called Stone Pavement, in Hebrew, Gabbatha. It was preparation day for Passover, and it was about noon. And he said to the Jews, "Behold, your king!" They cried out, "Take him away, take him away! Crucify him!" Pilate said to them, "Shall I crucify your king?" The chief priests answered, "We have no king but Caesar." Then he handed him over to them to be crucified.

So they took Jesus, and, carrying the cross himself, he went out to what is called the Place of the Skull, in Hebrew, Golgotha. There they crucified him, and with him two others, one on either side, with Jesus in the middle. Pilate also had an inscription written and put on the cross. It read, "Jesus the Nazorean, the King of the Jews." Now many of the Jews read this inscription, because the place where Jesus was crucified was near the city; and it was written in Hebrew, Latin, and Greek. So the chief priests of the Jews said to Pilate, "Do not write 'The King of the Jews,' but that he said, 'I am the King of the Jews'." Pilate answered, "What I have written, I have written."

When the soldiers had crucified Jesus, they took his clothes and divided them into four shares, a share for each soldier. They also took his tunic, but the tunic was seamless, woven in one piece from the top down. So they said to one another, "Let's not tear it, but cast lots for it to see whose it will be," in order that the passage of Scripture might be fulfilled that says:
They divided my garments among them,
and for my vesture they cast lots.
This is what the soldiers did. Standing by the cross of Jesus were his mother and his mother's sister, Mary the wife of Clopas, and Mary of Magdala. When Jesus saw his mother and the disciple there whom he loved he said to his mother, "Woman, behold, your son." Then he said to the disciple, "Behold, your mother." And from that hour the disciple took her into his home.

After this, aware that everything was now finished, in order that the Scripture might be fulfilled, Jesus said, "I thirst." There was a vessel filled with common wine. So they put a sponge soaked in wine on a sprig of hyssop and put it up to his mouth. When Jesus had taken the wine, he said, "It is finished." And bowing his head, he handed over the spirit.

Here all kneel and pause for a short time.

Now since it was preparation day, in order that the bodies might not remain on the cross on the sabbath, for the sabbath day of that week was a solemn one, the Jews asked Pilate that their legs be broken and that they be taken down. So the soldiers came and broke the legs of the first and then of the other one who was crucified with Jesus. But when they came to Jesus and saw that he was already dead, they did not break his legs, but one soldier thrust his lance into his side, and immediately blood and water flowed out. An eyewitness has testified, and his testimony is true; he knows that he is speaking the truth, so that you also may come to believe. For this happened so that the Scripture passage might be fulfilled:
Not a bone of it will be broken.
And again another passage says:
They will look upon him whom they have pierced.

After this, Joseph of Arimathea, secretly a disciple of Jesus for fear of the Jews, asked Pilate if he could remove the body of Jesus. And Pilate permitted it. So he came and took his body. Nicodemus, the one who had first come to him at night, also came bringing a mixture of myrrh and aloes weighing about one hundred pounds. They took the body of Jesus and bound it with burial cloths along with the spices, according to the Jewish burial custom. Now in the place where he had been crucified there was a garden, and in the garden a new tomb, in which no one had yet been buried. So they laid Jesus there because of the Jewish preparation day; for the tomb was close by.

Friends, our Gospel today is John's great account of the Passion of Jesus. The ultimate good—God incarnate—appeared, and we collectively responded not with exultation but with murderous violence. On Calvary, the Author of Life was crucified and killed.

The Crucifixion is the fullest expression of the divine anger at sin. We are meant to see on that cross, not simply a violent display, but rather our own ugliness. What brought Jesus to the cross? Stupidity, anger, mistrust, institutional injustice, betrayal of friends, denial, unspeakable cruelty, scapegoating, and fear.

But in the brutality of the cross we also see the fullest expression of the divine solidarity with sinners. God himself has come to stand with us in our dysfunction and absorb into his forgiveness all of the deadly sins. Yes, we know, with disquieting certitude, that we are sinners. But with Paul, we willingly boast of our weakness, for we know with equal clarity that we are redeemed sinners.

Jesus' Crucifixion was the opening up of the divine heart so that we could see that no sin of ours could finally separate us from the love of God.

REFLECT: Why does the sacrificial death of Jesus on the cross showcase the greatest love?

_____

_____

_____

_____

_____

_____

_____

_____

_____

Saturday, April 3, 2021

Holy Saturday

When the sabbath was over, Mary Magdalene, Mary, the mother of James, and Salome bought spices so that they might go and anoint him. Very early when the sun had risen, on the first day of the week, they came to the tomb. They were saying to one another, "Who will roll back the stone for us from the entrance to the tomb?" When they looked up, they saw that the stone had been rolled back; it was very large. On entering the tomb they saw a young man sitting on the right side, clothed in a white robe, and they were utterly amazed. He said to them, "Do not be amazed! You seek Jesus of Nazareth, the crucified. He has been raised; he is not here. Behold the place where they laid him. But go and tell his disciples and Peter, 'He is going before you to Galilee; there you will see him, as he told you.'"

LENTEN *GOSPEL* REFLECTIONS

Friends, on this Holy Saturday in our Gospel we hear St. Mark's account of the Resurrection. The Resurrection of Jesus from the dead is the be-all and end-all of the Christian faith. If Jesus didn't rise from the dead, all bishops, priests, and Christian ministers should go home and get honest jobs, and all the Christian faithful should leave their churches immediately.

As Paul himself put it: ""If Christ has not been raised, then empty is our preaching; empty, too, your faith. . . . If for this life only we have hoped in Christ, we are the most pitiable people of all." It's no good, of course, trying to explain the Resurrection away or rationalize it as a myth, a symbol, or an inner subjective experience. None of that does justice to the novelty and sheer strangeness of the biblical message.

It comes down finally to this: if Jesus was not raised from death, Christianity is a fraud and a joke. But if he did rise from death, then Christianity is the fullness of God's revelation, and Jesus must be the absolute center of our lives. There is no third option.

REFLECT: Why does St. Paul in his First Letter to the Corinthians say that if Christ has not been raised, your faith is "empty"?

_____

_____

_____

_____

_____

_____

_____

Sunday, April 4, 2021

Easter Sunday: The Resurrection of the Lord

On the first day of the week, Mary of Magdala came to the tomb early in the morning, while it was still dark, and saw the stone removed from the tomb. So she ran and went to Simon Peter and to the other disciple whom Jesus loved, and told them, "They have taken the Lord from the tomb, and we don't know where they put him." So Peter and the other disciple went out and came to the tomb. They both ran, but the other disciple ran faster than Peter and arrived at the tomb first; he bent down and saw the burial cloths there, but did not go in. When Simon Peter arrived after him, he went into the tomb and saw the burial cloths there, and the cloth that had covered his head, not with the burial cloths but rolled up in a separate place. Then the other disciple also went in, the one who had arrived at the tomb first, and he saw and believed. For they did not yet understand the Scripture that he had to rise from the dead.

Friends, our Easter Gospel contains St. John's magnificent account of the Resurrection.

Three key lessons follow from the disquieting fact of the Resurrection. First, this world is not all there is. The Resurrection of Jesus from the dead shows as definitively as possible that God is up to something greater than we had imagined. We don't have to live as though death were our master and as though nihilism were the only coherent point of view. We can, in fact, begin to see this world as a place of gestation toward something higher, more permanent, more splendid.

Second, the tyrants know that their time is up. Remember that the cross was Rome's way of asserting its authority. But when Jesus was raised from the dead through the power of the Holy Spirit, the first Christians knew that Caesar's days were, in point of fact, numbered. The faculty lounge interpretation of the Resurrection as a subjective event or a mere symbol is exactly what the tyrants of the world want, for it poses no real threat to them.

Third, the path of salvation has been opened to everyone. Jesus went all the way down, journeying into pain, despair, alienation, even godforsakenness. He went as far as you can go away from the Father. Why? In order to reach all those who had wandered from God. In light of the Resurrection, the first Christians came to know that, even as we run as fast as we can away from the Father, we are running into the arms of the Son.

Let us not domesticate these still-stunning lessons of the Resurrection. Rather, let us allow them to unnerve us, change us, and set us on fire.

REFLECT: Why is the Resurrection really the startling "good news" of the Gospel? How does it give you hope to celebrate it today?

STATIONS OF
THE CROSS
REFLECTIONS

*To watch the video and download the audio version
of these Stations of the Cross, visit:*
Stations.WordOnFire.org

*The biblical verses in the **Stations of the Cross Reflections** were transcribed
from Bishop Barron's oral presentation and may not match a specific
translation exactly.*

Jesus Is Condemned to Death

When Israel dreamed of a new David, it dreamed of a king who would unite the nation, cleanse the temple, defeat Israel's enemies, and then reign over the whole world. It's only against this loamy backdrop that we can appreciate what Jesus was doing and how he was perceived. The first words out of his mouth—and the central theme of his preaching—concerned the kingdom of God. He announced a new reign, centered on himself.

These were taken, quite rightly, as fighting words, for if a new kingdom is to come, the old kingdoms have to give way, and if a new King has arrived, the old kings have to cede. Jesus endeavored to unite the nation, to bring the tribes back together. This was the point of his open-table fellowship, his reaching out to sinners and tax collectors, his inclusion of the sick and the marginalized. In David's city, he cleansed the temple and promised that he would establish a new temple. And throughout his life and ministry, Jesus opposed the old kings. We see it from the very beginning, in the infancy narratives themselves. Jesus is presented as an alternative to Quirinius and Augustus, and his arrival, even as a baby, is enough to frighten Herod and all Jerusalem.

This confrontation between the old and new orders comes to its highest expression as Jesus stands before Pontius Pilate, the local representative of Caesar. Pilate, undoubtedly sure of his power and authority, sizes up this criminal: "Are you the King of the Jews?" Pilate means this in a purely political and worldly way: "Are

3

you trying to seize political control of this part of the Roman empire?" But the scene is packed with irony, for any Jew would have known the full import of Pilate's question. He was really asking: "Are you the king of the world? Are you the new David, destined to reign over all of the nations?"

Jesus tells him, straightforwardly enough, "My kingdom does not belong to this world." This does not mean that Jesus is unconcerned for the realities of politics, with the very "this-worldly" concerns of justice, peace, and right order. It means that the reign that he has been announcing is not a new political order, based like the others on threats and violence. This is why he immediately clarifies that his attendants are not "fighting to keep me from being handed over." It is the reign of God that he announces, God's nonviolent and compassionate ordering of things. Unimpressed, Pilate asks, "What is truth?" And then he condemns Jesus to death. He plays the typical worldly game of power politics, and by all appearances, he wins, as ruthless and violent people seem to do.

But through the cross and Resurrection, Jesus defeated him. He outmaneuvered the violence of sin and swallowed it up in the divine forgiveness. He defeated the enemies of Israel. And he thereby established his own body as the new temple—which is why blood and water flowed out from it. He gathered all people to himself, as the Davidic king was expected to: "When the Son of man is raised up, he will draw all people to himself." He was, in short, the new King, the one to whom final allegiance is due.

Jesus Takes Up His Cross

STATION II

All of us sinners tend to see the universe turning around our egos, our needs, our projects, our plans, our likes and dislikes. True conversion—the *metanoia* that Jesus talks about—is so much more than moral reform, though it includes that. It has to do with a complete shift in consciousness, a whole new way of looking at one's life.

Jesus offered a teaching that must have been gut-wrenching to his first-century audience: "If anyone wishes to come after me, he must deny himself and take up his cross daily and follow me." His listeners knew what the cross meant: a death in utter agony, nakedness, and humiliation. They knew it in all of its awful power.

So why does the Son take up the cross? Because God the Father is angry? Because he wants to lord it over us? Because God needs something? No, he comes purely out of love, out of God's desire that we flourish: "God so loved the world that he gave his only Son, so that everyone who believes in him might not perish but might have eternal life." God the Father is not a pathetic divinity whose bruised personal honor needs to be restored; rather, God is a parent who burns with compassion for his children who have wandered into danger. Does the Father hate sinners? No, but he hates sin. Does he harbor indignation at the unjust? No, but he despises injustice. And thus he sends his Son—not to see him suffer but to set things right. St. Anselm, the great medieval theologian who is often unfairly blamed for the cruel theology of satisfaction, was eminently clear on this score. We sinners are like diamonds that have fallen into the muck; made in the image of God, we have soiled ourselves through violence and hatred. In his passion to reestablish the beauty of his creation, God came down into the muck of sin and death and brought the diamond up and polished it off. In so doing of course, he had to get dirty. This sinking into the dirt—this divine solidarity with the lost—is the "sacrifice" that the Son makes to the infinite pleasure of the Father. It is a sacrifice expressive not of anger or vengeance but of compassion.

If God is self-forgetting love even to the point of death, then we must be such love. If God is willing to break open his own heart, then we must be willing to break open our hearts for others. The cross, in short, must become the very structure of the Christian life.

There's a line from the illuminator of the St. John's Bible that states: "We have to love our way out of this." There's nothing wimpy or namby-pamby or blind about this conviction. When we love extravagantly, we are not purposely blinding ourselves to moral realities—just the contrary. Love is not a sentiment but "a harsh and dreadful thing," as Dostoevsky said.

This is just what Jesus shows on his terrible cross. And this is just what we, his followers, must imitate. Taking up the cross means not just being willing to suffer but being willing to suffer as he did, absorbing violence and hatred through our forgiveness and nonviolence.

Jesus Falls for the First Time

On the way to Calvary, Jesus—the Son of God—fell under the weight of the cross.

Some years ago, I delivered a homily on the subject of God's benevolent and providential direction of the cosmos. I felt the sermon had been inspiring and informative, and the numerous people who complimented me afterward confirmed my own assessment. But after everybody else had streamed past me, an older man approached, and eyeing me warily, said, "Father, I'm on a quest, and your homily didn't help." I responded, "Well, what do you mean?"

He then proceeded to tell me a terrible story. He had two granddaughters, ages five and seven, both of whom were suffering from a terminal disease that the doctors could neither control nor fully understand. All they knew for sure was that both girls would die and that, before death, both would go blind. He told me that the elder child had just lost her sight and that the younger was lying awake at night crying in terror as she contemplated her own future. "Father," he said, "my quest is to find out why God is doing this to my granddaughters. I've been to priests, ministers, rabbis, and gurus, and I've never gotten a very good answer— and frankly, your homily shed very little light." Well, I was flabbergasted, stunned. Never had the problem of evil—reconciling the goodness of God with the presence of suffering—appeared to me so concretely and in such a challenging way.

I told him that I didn't have a concrete answer to his question, but that his question itself was a holy

9

one, because it meant that he had not given up on God. He was still searching for God. And if you follow that question all the way, you'll be led to the heart of the Christian mystery, which is that God the Father sends his Son into the very worst of our suffering, into what frightens us the most. And in that we have the answer—not necessarily one that satisfies our curiosity completely, but a deeply powerful spiritual answer: that God doesn't take away our suffering, but he enters into it with us and thereby sanctifies it.

Jesus Meets His Blessed Mother

The Passion of the Christ was one of the most provocative and popular religious movies in decades. One thing that especially struck me when I saw it is the role played by Mary, the mother of Jesus. We are compelled to see the scenes through her eyes. Early in Luke's Gospel, we are told that Mary "contemplated these things, reflecting on them in her heart." She is the theologian par excellence. She is the one who understands.

If Mary is the one through whom Christ was born, and if the Church is indeed Christ's Mystical Body, then she must be, in a very real sense, the Mother of the Church. She is the one through whom Jesus continues to be born. We hear in the Gospel that, as he was dying on the cross, Jesus looked to his mother and the disciple whom he loved, and he said to Mary, "Woman, behold, your son," then to John, "Behold, your mother." We are told that "from that hour the disciple took her into his home." This text supports an ancient tradition that the Apostle John would have taken Mary with him when he traveled to Ephesus in Asia Minor and that both ended their days in that city. Indeed, on the top of a high hill overlooking the Aegean Sea, just outside of Ephesus, there's a modest dwelling that tradition holds to be the house of Mary. Immaculate Mary, the Mother of God, assumed body and soul into heaven, is not of merely historical or theoretical interest, nor is she simply a spiritual exemplar. Instead, as "Queen of all the saints," Mary is an ongoing presence, an actor in the life of the Church. In entrusting Mary to John, Jesus was, in a real way, entrusting Mary to all those who would be friends of Jesus down through the ages.

This is not to confuse her, of course, with the Savior, but it is to insist on her mission as mediator and intercessor. At the close of the great "Hail Mary" prayer, we Catholics ask Mary to pray for us "now and at the hour of our death," signaling that throughout one's life, Mary is the privileged channel through which the grace of Christ flows into the Mystical Body. Her basic task is always to draw people into deeper fellowship with her son. The Church's conviction is that the Blessed Mother continues to say yes to God and to "go in haste" on mission around the world. She does so usually in quiet, hidden ways, responding to prayer and interceding for the Church. But sometimes she does so in a remarkable manner, breaking into our world strikingly and visibly.

God delights in drawing secondary causes into the dense complexity of his providential plan, granting to them the honor of cooperating with him and his designs. The Virgin Mary, the handmaid of the Lord, is the humblest of these humble instruments—and therefore, the most effective.

Simon of Cyrene Is Made to Help Jesus Bear the Cross

A donkey is a beast of burden: a humble, simple, unassuming animal, used by very ordinary people to do their work. The wealthy and powerful might own horses or a team of oxen; a political leader might ride a stately steed; but they would have little to do with donkeys.

All of his public career, Jesus had resisted when people claimed Messiahship for him. He sternly ordered them to be silent. When they came to carry him off and make him king, he slipped away. But on Palm Sunday, he is willing to be proclaimed—precisely at the moment when he rides into Jerusalem on a donkey. And the Gospel is clear: it is a colt, the foal of a donkey, on whom no one had ever previously sat. In other words, this is a young, inexperienced, unimpressive donkey. And this is the animal upon whom Jesus rides into town in triumph.

The humble donkey, pressed into service, is a model of discipleship. Our purpose in life is not to draw attention to ourselves, to have a brilliant career, to aggrandize our egos; rather, our purpose is to serve the Master's need, to cooperate with his work as he sees fit. What was the donkey's task? He was a Christopher, a Christ-bearer. He carried the Lord into Jerusalem, paving the way for the Passion and the redemption of the world. Would anyone have particularly noticed him? Probably not, except perhaps to laugh at this ludicrous animal. What is the task of every disciple? Just the same: to be a Christopher, a bearer of Christ to the world. Might we be unnoticed in this? Sure. Might we, if we are noticed, be laughed at? Well, of course. But the Master has need of us, and so we perform our essential task in the theo-drama.

During Christ's Passion, there is one figure who imitates the donkey, and that's Simon of Cyrene. The Romans didn't want Jesus to die before the Crucifixion. And so they pressed into service (how like the donkey!) a man from Cyrene, in North Africa, probably a visitor coming to Jerusalem for the Passover.

How perilous and dangerous this must have seemed to him! But he seizes the moment and carries the cross, bearing some of Jesus' suffering. Simon of Cyrene must have had many other plans for his life, many other dreams and ambitions. But at the moment of truth, the Master had need of him—and he responded.

And his story is told to this day. "Life is what happens to you while you're busy making other plans." Your life is not about you. Remember: the Master has need of you. Whether and how you respond is all that matters.

Veronica Wipes the Face of Jesus

Tradition has it that a woman called Veronica wiped the blood and sweat from Jesus' face as he made his way to Calvary, leaving his image miraculously imprinted on her veil.

What do we see in the face of Christ? We see the Son of God, the divine Word made flesh. To use Paul's language, God has brought to light "the knowledge of the glory of God on the face of Jesus Christ." In and through his humble humanity, his divinity shines forth. The proximity of his divinity in no way compromises the integrity of his humanity but rather makes it shine in greater beauty. This is the New Testament version of the burning bush. The Jesus who is both divine and human is the Jesus who is evangelically compelling. If he is only divine, then he doesn't touch us; if he is only human, he can't save us. His splendor consists in the coming together of the two natures. This is the Christ who wants to reign as Lord of our lives in every detail.

And we see, in the veil of Veronica, the suffering Lamb of God who takes away the sins of the world. The Lord of Life came, and we killed him. Therefore hiding, denying, covering up, pretense, excuses, subterfuges— all the ruses of self-justification—are permanently out of the question. Our own dysfunction is on public view in every wound on the body of Jesus. When we direct ourselves toward the brilliance of the crucified Christ, every smudge on the windowpane of the soul becomes visible. In the tormented face of the suffering Christ, we know that something has gone terribly wrong with us; that no one is okay; that we're like prisoners chained inside of an escape-proof prison; that we are at war with ourselves; that Pharaoh has enslaved the Israelites and pressed them into service; that we are under judgment; that all we can do is cry, "O Come, O Come, Emmanuel."

But in that veil of Veronica, we also see the face of mercy. When we had wandered into the cold and distant country of sin, God's love came to search us out; when we had sunk under the waves, that love went deeper; when we had closed ourselves up in the somber cave of our self-regard and self-reproach, that love crouched down, and with a candle, entered in. And this is why we Christians don't hide the awful face of the dying Christ. This is why we show it to the world. In Jesus' agonies, God is taking our agony away. We know it is no longer we who live but Christ who lives in us; we realize that nothing can ever separate us from the love of God. The Church doesn't have a mission; it is a mission, and its purpose is to cause the merciful face of Jesus to gaze upon everyone in the world.

Jesus Falls for the Second Time

Under the crushing weight of the cross, Jesus fell a second time.

The prophet Jeremiah gave voice to a longing and a hope that must have been deeply planted in the collective consciousness of the nation. He expresses Yahweh's own pledge that he himself would one day fulfill the covenant and forgive the sins of the people. In the thirty-first chapter of the book of Jeremiah, we find these extraordinary words: "The days are surely coming, says the Lord, when I will make a new covenant with the house of Israel and the house of Judah. It will not be like the covenant I made with their ancestors . . . a covenant that they broke. . . . But this is the covenant that I will make with the house of Israel after those days. . . . I will put my law within them, and I will write it on their hearts; and I will be their God and they will be my people." All the prophets know that the covenants God made with Israel—through Abraham, Moses, and David—have failed, due to the people's infidelity. But Jeremiah dreams that one day, through Yahweh's own direct intervention, a faithful Israel will emerge, a people who have a heart for the Lord, who consider the Law not an external imposition but a joy.

How will this renewal take place? How will Yahweh plant the Law so deeply in the children of Israel that their fulfillment of the covenant will be effortless? To find the answers, we must turn to some mysterious texts in the book of the prophet Isaiah, texts that particularly fascinated the first Christians. In the fifty-second chapter of Isaiah, we find a reference to a figure called "the servant of the Lord," who, we are told, "will be exalted and lifted up and shall be very high." The nations of the earth will see him in this prominent position, but they shall not be looking at a splendid warrior or a majestic victor. Instead, they will be astonished at how "marred was his appearance, beyond human semblance." In chapter fifty-three, the description of this servant continues: "He had no form or majesty that we should look at him, nothing in his appearance that we should desire him. He was despised and rejected by others, a man of suffering and acquainted with infirmity." And then the reason for his deformation and anguish is made clearer: "Surely, he has borne our infirmities and carried our diseases. . . . He was wounded for our transgressions, crushed for our iniquities . . . and the Lord has laid on him the iniquity of us all."

The "suffering servant" is presented, in short, as a sacrificial figure, one who will, on behalf of the entire nation, offer himself for the sins of the many. His greatness will consist not in personal independence and political power but rather in his willingness to bear the weight of sin, to disempower sin, as it were, from within. In a word, the covenant of which Jeremiah speaks (the writing of the Law in the hearts of the people) would be effected through the sacrificial servant of whom Isaiah speaks.

Jesus Meets the Women of Jerusalem

As Jesus is led to Calvary, a great number followed him, including weeping women of Jerusalem. Jesus turned to them and spoke as judge of the world, saying, "Daughters of Jerusalem, do not weep for me, but weep for yourselves and for your children."

The New Testament insists that Jesus both shows us that we are sinners (he is judge) and offers us the way out of sin (he is savior). When one or the other of these emphases is lost, our spiritual path is decisively compromised, either through overconfidence or through terror. When they are both adequately stressed, our spiritual path opens up, because we know we must walk it and we can walk it.

In Jesus of Nazareth, God's own mind became flesh—that is to say, the pattern of God's being appeared in time and space. Colossians tells us that Jesus is the "perfect image," the *eikon*, of the Father. And thus, his arrival was in itself a challenge to all that is not in conformity with the divine pattern. In his very person is the kingdom, the divine *ordo*, and therefore his presence is the light in which the disorder of all the earthly kingdoms becomes apparent. In this sense, his every move, his every word, his every gesture, constituted God's judgment on the world, for in the measure that he was opposed, he clarified the dysfunctional nature of his opponents. When John the Baptist spoke of the coming of the Messiah, he used an edgy image: "His winnowing fork is in his hand, to clear his threshing floor and to gather the wheat into the granary; but the chaff he will burn with unquenchable fire." The farmer in first-century Palestine would place the newly harvested wheat on the floor of the barn and then, using a sort of pitchfork, would toss the grain in the air, forcing the lighter chaff to separate itself from the usable wheat. Thus Jesus' presence would be a winnowing fan, an agent of separation and clarification.

And nowhere is this judgment more evident than in his violent death. Jesus did not simply pass away; he was killed, executed by command of the Roman governor and with the approval of the religious establishment. As Peter put it in the earliest kerygmatic preaching in the Acts of the Apostles: "And you killed the Author of life, whom God raised from the dead." The implication of Peter's speech, of course, is that you, the killers, have been revealed as the enemies of life. And the "you," as Peter himself knew with special insight, included not simply the Roman and Jewish ruling classes, but everyone, even Jesus' most intimate followers.

All the social groups of Jesus' time—Pharisees, Sadducees, Zealots, Essenes, temple priests, Roman occupiers, Christian disciples—had this in common: they were, at the end of the day, opposed to Jesus. At the moment of truth, "they all fled." Bob Dylan said, "The enemy I see / wears the cloak of decency." A favorite ruse of sinners is to wrap themselves in the mantle of respectability; Jesus the judge is the one who rips away the cloak, literally unveiling, "revealing" the truth of things. Whenever we are tempted to think that all is well with us, we hold up the cross of Jesus and let our illusions die.

Jesus Falls for the Third Time

Why did Jesus bear the terrible weight of the cross—a cross so heavy it caused him to fall not once, not twice, but three times?

Because if the weight of sin had been addressed only from a distance, only through divine fiat, it would not have been truly conquered; but when it is withstood by someone willing fully to submit to it, it is effectively exploded from within, undermined, defeated. This is the strategy of Jesus, the Lamb of God.

We see it in a number of Gospel scenes where Jesus is tired out after his contact with the sick, the lost, the sinful. At the beginning of Mark's Gospel, we find an account of a typical day in the ministry of Jesus. The people press on him from all sides, compelling him to find refuge in a boat lest he be crushed by the crowd, and at one point there are so many supplicants surrounding him that he couldn't even eat. Mark tells us that Jesus went off to a secluded place to pray, but even there they sought him out, coming at him from all sides.

In the magnificent narrative of the woman at the well in the Gospel of John, we hear that Jesus sat down by Jacob's well, "tired out by his journey." This description is straightforward enough on the literal level: Who wouldn't be tired after a morning's march through dry country? But as Augustine and others have reminded us, it has another sense on the mystical level. Jesus is tired from his incarnational journey into human sin and dysfunction, signified by the well. "You come to this well every day and you become thirsty again," Jesus says to the woman, indicating that the well is emblematic of errant desire, her tendency to fill up her longing for God with the transient goods of creation: money, pleasure, power, honor. In order to effect a change in her, the Lamb of God had to be willing to enter into her dysfunctional world and to share the spiritual weariness of it. J.R.R. Tolkien keenly appreciated this sacrificial dynamic. His great Christ-figure, Frodo the hobbit, brought about the salvation of Middle-earth precisely through his entry into the heart of the land of Mordor, disempowering that terrible place through his humble willingness to bear the full weight of its burden.

All of this was, however, but an anticipation of the ultimate sacrifice of the Lamb of God. The final enemy that had to be defeated, if God and his human family could once again sit down in easy fellowship, was death itself. In a very real sense, death—and the fear of death—stand behind all sin, and hence Jesus had to journey into the realm of death and, through sacrifice, twist it back to life. Innumerable heroes in the course of human history had tried to conquer that realm by using its weapons, fighting violence with violence and hatred with hatred. But this strategy was (and still is) hopeless. The battle plan of the Lamb of God was paradoxical in the extreme: he would conquer death precisely by dying.

Jesus is Stripped of His Garments

The soldiers took Jesus' clothes and divided them into four shares, a share for each soldier, and cast lots for his tunic, fulfilling the words of the Psalms: "They divided my garments among them, and for my vesture they cast lots." Christ is stripped of everything: reputation, comfort, esteem, food, drink—even the pathetic clothes on his back.

Thomas Aquinas said that if you want to see the perfect exemplification of the beatitudes, you should look to Christ crucified. He specified this observation as follows: if you want beatitude (happiness), despise what Jesus despised on the cross and love what he loved on the cross.

What did he despise on the cross but the four classical addictions—wealth, pleasure, power, and honor? At the root of sin is fear, especially fear of death. To counter that fear, people aggrandize the ego, decorating it with the approval of others or stuffing it with worldly goods. But the crucified Jesus was utterly detached from wealth and worldly goods. He was stripped naked, and his hands, fixed to the wood of the cross, could grasp at nothing. More to it, he was detached from pleasure. On the cross, Jesus underwent the most agonizing kind of physical torment, a pain that was literally excruciating (*ex cruce*, from the cross), but he also experienced the extreme of psychological and even spiritual suffering. And he was bereft of power, even to the point of being unable to move or defend himself in any way. Finally, on that terrible cross, he was completely detached from the esteem of others. In a public place not far from the gate of Jerusalem, he hung from an instrument of torture, exposed to the mockery of the crowd, displayed as a common criminal. In this, he endured the limit case of dishonor. In the most dramatic way possible, therefore, the crucified Jesus demonstrated a liberation from the four principal temptations that lead us from God. St. Paul expressed this accomplishment in typically vivid language: "He nailed our sins to the cross."

But what did Jesus love on the cross? He loved the will of his Father. His Father had sent him into the farthest reaches of godforsakenness in order to bring the divine love even to that darkest place, and Jesus loved that mission to the very end. And it was precisely his detachment from the four great temptations that enabled him to walk that walk. What he loved and what he despised were in a strange balance on the cross. Poor in spirit, meek, mourning, and persecuted, he was able to be pure of heart, to seek righteousness utterly, to become the ultimate peacemaker, and to be the perfect conduit of the divine mercy to the world. Though it is supremely paradoxical to say so, the crucified Jesus is, therefore, the man of beatitude, a truly happy man. And Jesus, stripped of his garments and nailed to the cross, is the very icon of liberty, for he is free from those attachments that would prevent him from attaining the true good, which is doing the will of his Father.

Jesus is Crucified

32

On the cross, Jesus said, "Father, forgive them, for they know not what they do." Dying on a Roman instrument of torture, he allowed the full force of the world's hatred and dysfunction to wash over him, to spend itself on him. And he responded not with an answering violence or resentment, but with forgiveness. He therefore took away the sin of the world (to use the language of the liturgy), swallowing it up in the divine mercy.

In the Gospel of Luke, Jesus compared himself to a mother hen who longed to gather her chicks under her wing. As N.T. Wright points out, this is much more than a sentimental image. It refers to the gesture of a hen when fire is sweeping through the barn. In order to protect her chicks, she will sacrifice herself, gathering them under her wing and using her own body as a shield. On the cross, Jesus used, as it were, his own sacrificed body as a shield, taking the full force of the world's hatred and violence. He entered into close quarters with sin (because that's where we sinners are found) and allowed the heat and fury of sin to destroy him, even as he protected us. With this metaphor in mind, we can see, with special clarity, why the first Christians associated the crucified Jesus with the suffering servant of Isaiah. By enduring the pain of the cross, Jesus did indeed bear our sins; by his stripes we were indeed healed.

Through the final sacrifice of Jesus the high priest, eternal life has been made available to the whole of humanity. The sacrifice of the Mass is a participation in this great eternal act by which Jesus entered on our behalf into the heavenly sanctuary with his own blood and returned bearing the forgiveness of the Father. When the high priest came out of the sanctuary and sprinkled the people with blood, he was understood to be acting in the very person of Yahweh, renewing creation. The ultimate sacrifice having been offered, Christ the priest comes forth at every Mass with his lifeblood, and the universe is restored. The priest's actions at the altar are but a symbolic manifestation of this mystical reality, which is why he is described as operating *in persona Christi* (in the person of Christ).

Though the ordained priest alone can preside at the Mass and effect the Eucharistic change, all of the baptized participate in the Mass in a priestly way. They do this through their prayers and responses but also, as *Lumen Gentium* specifies, by uniting their personal sacrifices and sufferings to the great sacrifice of Christ. So a father witnesses the agony of his son in the hospital; a mother endures the rebellion of a teenage daughter; a young man receives news of his brother's death in battle; an elderly man tosses on his bed in anxiety as he contemplates his unsure financial situation; a graduate student struggles to complete his doctoral thesis; a child experiences for the first time the breakup of a close friendship; an idealist confronts the stubborn resistance of a cynical opponent. These people could see their pain as simply dumb suffering, the offscourings of an indifferent universe. Or they could see them through the lens provided by the sacrificial death of Jesus, appreciating them as the means by which God is drawing them closer to himself.

Jesus Dies on the Cross

In Mark's Gospel, the last thing we hear from Jesus is an animal cry: "Jesus gave a loud cry and breathed his last." But in John's Gospel, in which the priesthood of Jesus is consistently emphasized, we find, just before Jesus' death, a liturgical word. In the Latin version of this passage, it is *consummatum est*: it is completed. This is the affirmation that a work has been done, that something has been brought to fulfillment. How often in the New Testament do we hear the language of fulfillment: "in order that the Scriptures might be fulfilled" and "in fulfillment of the Scriptures." Jesus saw himself as the climax of a story, as the culminating chapter in a novel, as the hinge of a great drama. If we don't know the contours of the drama, we won't know him.

And the drama involves a rescue operation that God launched by forming the people of Israel after his own heart. When the world had gone wrong through sin, God endeavored to fashion a family that would know him and would worship him aright. This process began with Abraham and the covenant that God cut with him. It continued through Moses and David, as God secured further covenants with them. He wanted to form a priestly people, a people of orthodoxy, right praise. This rightly-ordered people would then become a magnet to the other nations of the world: "Mt. Zion, true pole of the earth, there all the tribes go up, the tribes of the Lord." Though God was ever faithful, the people Israel wavered. Though they were called back by the prophets to covenant fidelity, they did not listen. Though the temple was established as the place of right praise, it became corrupt. And Israel was not the magnet for the other nations but rather their footstool and servant. Israel was enslaved by Egypt, overrun by Assyria, Babylon, Greece, and Rome. More to it, the tribes of Israel, instead of coming together around Mt. Zion, had been scattered. And so Israel began to dream of a new King David, a figure who would fulfill all of its expectations and complete God's rescue operation.

The author of John's Gospel was a master of irony, and one of his most delicious twists involves the sign that Pontius Pilate placed over the cross of the dying Jesus: *Iesus Nazarenus Rex Iudaeorum* (Jesus of Nazareth, King of the Jews). The Roman governor, of course, meant it as a taunt, but the sign—written out in the three major languages of that time and place, Hebrew, Latin, and Greek—in fact made Pilate, unwittingly, the first great evangelist. The king of the Jews, on the Old Testament reading, was destined to be the king of the world—and this is precisely what Pilate effectively announced. Even at Calvary, when it had dwindled to three members, Jesus' Church, his community, was catholic, for it was destined to embrace everyone. At Pentecost, the disciples, gathered in the Upper Room, were filled with the Holy Spirit and began to preach the Good News. They were heard, miraculously, in the many languages of those who had gathered in Jerusalem for the Feast of Tabernacles. As the Church Fathers clearly saw, this was the reversal of the curse of Babel, when the one language of the human race was divided and the people, accordingly, set against each other. Now, through the announcement of the Lordship of Jesus, the many languages again become one, for this message is the one that every person, across space and time, was born to hear: Jesus is the new King.

Jesus Is Taken Down from the Cross and Laid in the Arms of Mary

After the Crucifixion, Jesus was taken from the Cross and laid in the arms of Mary—a scene famously captured in Michelangelo's iconic *Pietà*.

For five centuries now, scholars and admirers have remarked the serenity and youthfulness of Mary's face in the *Pietà*. Mary, we presume, would have been at least forty-five or fifty at the time of the Crucifixion. And yet, Michelangelo depicts her as a young woman, perhaps in her early twenties.

What Michelangelo was showing us is not only the historical Mary, but Mary as new Eve, an ever-young Mother of the Church. Michelangelo was, throughout his life, a great devotee of the poet Dante. At the end of the *Divine Comedy* we find a famous line, placed on the lips of St. Bernard as he sings the praises of the Mother of God: "Virgin mother, daughter of your Son, humbled, and exalted, more than any other creature." Since Mary's son, according to the flesh, is also the divine Word through whom all things are made, Mary is indeed both mother and daughter of Christ. Michelangelo suggested this absolutely unique relationship in the youthfulness of Jesus' mother.

One of the most extraordinary features of the *Pietà*, from a purely structural or compositional standpoint, is how Michelangelo managed to make the figures of Jesus and Mary look so natural and elegant together, despite the fact that what is being presented is a woman supporting the body of an adult man on her lap. In fact, Mary's body is significantly larger than that of Jesus. She contains him. In the wonderful words of Sister Wendy

Beckett, she's like a great mountain, and his body is like a river flowing down. The Church Fathers compared Mary to the ark of the covenant, the receptacle of the Ten Commandments, which the ancient Israelites appreciated as the dwelling place of God. So Mary, who carried the incarnate Word in her very womb, becomes the Ark of the Covenant par excellence.

According to the Gospel accounts, Mary, having given birth to Jesus, placed him in a manger, the place where the animals eat. At the climax of his life, Jesus would become food for the life of the world. Michelangelo depicts Mary's left hand in a gesture of offering, as though she is presenting him as a gift. (This same gesture is found in that especially evocative scene in *The Passion of the Christ* when Mary, marked with Jesus' Blood, presents the sacrifice of her Son to us and for us.) Her right hand supports him but touches him only indirectly, through her garment. Both are Eucharistic references. The Church continually offers the Body of Jesus under the forms of bread and wine. And when the priest shows the Blessed Sacrament, he touches the monstrance only through a veil. Keep in mind that the sculpture was intended to be an altarpiece—that is to say, something closely associated with the celebration of the Mass. What we see in the *Pietà*, the image of the Virgin Mother cradling her Son, is what we see at the Mass—namely, the offering of the body of the crucified Jesus for the life of the world.

Jesus Is Laid in the Tomb

STATION XIV

Joseph of Arimathea, a secret admirer of Jesus, came courageously to ask for the body of the Lord, and a group of women who had accompanied Jesus from Galilee watched carefully to see where he was buried. As his enemies closed in on him and even his most intimate disciples fled in fear, these people stayed with Jesus until the end. Luke aptly speaks of the women as having "followed" the body of Jesus to its resting place, their discipleship of the Lord complete and consistent. Jesus wants to go to the cross because he loves his Father's will; and therefore, those who love him—who want what he wants—go to that same bitter end. In St. John's Gospel, we hear that Jesus is buried in a new tomb that was situated in a garden, which signals the renewal of Eden, the way back into the garden from which we were exiled through sin.

The three women come as we might expect any visitor to any grave to come: they have their oil with them, and they intend to honor the body of Jesus. We might imagine them sitting in reverential silence afterward, reflecting on the life and words of their friend, expressing their admiration for him and the tragedy of his death.

But this is no ordinary grave. The first thing they notice is the stone rolled away. Now, this could have been the result of grave-robbers, of someone trying to break in and desecrate the tomb. It is just beginning to dawn on them that it is the result of someone breaking out.

Then it says, "They made their way out and fled

from the tomb bewildered and trembling, and because of their great fear, they said nothing to anyone." This grave is not the source of peace and rest, calm and thoughtful meditation. This grave is the source of terror and upheaval. Ordinary graves are places of finality and inevitability; this grave is a place of novelty so shocking that it frightens the wits out of people. From this grave of Jesus, we learn that the supposed laws of nature aren't laws after all, that what always moved this way now moves that way. Some people think that they will make the Resurrection more intelligible, more acceptable to modern people, if they allegorize it away, turning it into a vague symbol of the perdurance of Jesus' cause. But then his grave wouldn't be frightening; it would be, like the grave of any ordinary hero, sad, wistful, reassuring.

Evangelization—the proclamation of the Good News, the Gospel, the *euangelion*—has to do with the Resurrection of Jesus Christ from the dead. On every page of the New Testament, one can discern an excitement born of something utterly novel and unexpected: that Jesus of Nazareth, who had died on a cross and was buried in a tomb, was, through the power of God, raised up.

Everything else in Christian life flows from and is related to this empty tomb.

All Stations of the Cross images are from the Church of All Saints in Blato, Korcula Island, Croatia.

Conclusion

Friends,

In the name of the Risen Lord, greetings! Lent is over and we've now moved into Easter. Alleluia!

I'd like to thank you for joining me on this journey through the Lenten season. Now that we've finished, you might be wondering, what's next? How do I maintain the spiritual momentum I developed during Lent? I'd like to suggest a few practical tips.

First, be sure to visit our website, **WordOnFire.org**, on a regular basis. There you'll find lots of helpful resources, including new articles, videos, blog posts, podcasts, and homilies, all designed to help strengthen your faith and evangelize the culture. The best part is that all of it is free!

In addition to those free resources, I invite you to join our new Word on Fire Institute. This is an online hub of deep spiritual and intellectual formation, where you'll journey through courses taught by me and other Fellows. Our goal is to build an army of evangelists, people who have been transformed by Christ and want to bring his light to the world. Learn more and sign up at **https://wordonfire.institute.**

Finally, consider carrying on your Lenten progress by grounding your life more concretely in the Eucharist, which is what keeps us alive spiritually. Are you only attending Mass on Sundays?

Commit to attending one extra Mass each week. Is there a chapel nearby that offers Eucharistic Adoration? Sign up for a weekly hour of meditation and prayer before the Blessed Sacrament. The Eucharist is the alpha and the omega of Christian discipleship. It is the energy without which authentic Christianity runs down.

Again, thank you from all of us at Word on Fire, and God bless you during this Easter season!

Peace,

+ Robert Barron

Bishop Robert Barron